CHANGING TIMES
NEW APPROACHES
A Handbook for Deacons

Jay van Groningen

CRC Publications / CRWRC   Grand Rapids, Michigan

Changing Times, New Approaches: A Handbook for Deacons, © 1996, CRC Publications, 2850 Kalamazoo Ave. SE, Grand Rapids, MI 49560.

ISBN 1-56212-222-3

Library of Congress Cataloging-in-Publication Data

Van Groningen, Jay, 1953-
    Changing times, new approaches : a handbook for deacons / Jay Van Groningen.
        p. cm.
    ISBN 1-56212-222-3
    1. Deacons. I. Title.
BV680.V26 1996
262'.145731—dc20   96-30771
                                                             CIP

10 9 8 7 6 5 4 3 2 1

Contents

Preface

Surveys tell us that deacons do a lot of benevolent work in their churches and connect quite well to community services such as food banks and other emergency resources. Long-term friendships between church members and needy community members are slowly beginning to grow, but their numbers are meager. And less than 2 percent of these people are enfolded into the church.

The facts speak for themselves. We are not reaching our communities for Christ. A radical shift in how we do our Savior's work is needed if, in fact, we are to fulfill His anointed calling, "to preach good news to the poor, . . . to proclaim the year of the Lord's favor" (Luke 4:18).

This book focuses on the mercy-ministry side of kingdom work—a natural and powerful means of effectively engaging our communities. Jay Van Groningen pictures for us a new vision for deacons. He calls the deacons and the diaconally minded to give the kind of leadership that will move the church beyond the handout stage of ministry. He envisions a ministry where individual church members are actively involved in the lives of those who are hurting and/or lost. He envisions a church that systemically addresses societal and institutional injustices. Poignant examples throughout the book illustrate that models that fulfill this vision already exist. We need to learn from these models and apply them on a wider scale.

Jay has been a blessing to the ministry of deacons. Since 1982, he has worked with the Christian Reformed World Relief Committee in ministry development in the U.S. The passion and understanding of this ministry come naturally to Jay. He grew up in Australia, where his family ministered to Asian students during a time when Australia had an unjust immigration ban on any Asians other than students. As a student at the Reformed Theological Seminary in Jackson, Mississippi, Jay taught catechism to teens in trouble. Now, as a regional director for CRWRC, responsible for an eleven-classis region, Jay still takes time to establish personal relationships with people who otherwise have been disenfranchised and neglected. He holds himself personally accountable for ministering to our communities' disadvantaged and introducing them to Christ. He desires that same accountability for the church at the local, classis, and national level.

This book is a call to action. It is also a guide that helps churches move down the road of engaging their communities. Additional resources are available through CRWRC and other agencies of the Christian Reformed Church of North America. Together we can proclaim good news to the poor of today!

Andy Ryskamp
Director of Diaconal Ministries, CRWRC

One: **Attending the Workers**

John was an energetic young man, eager to develop himself and make his mark in life. He worked hard to establish himself in his own law office and put in the long hours required to make a new law practice viable. Working with some of his clients brought a great deal of stress into John's life.

John had been married for a few years; his priority was a strong and growing relationship with his wife. John put a lot of effort into strengthening his marriage and family life. He spent time with his wife, and together they looked forward to having children.

His favorite hobby was sailing. He spent every available weekend in fair weather sailing with his wife and extended family. They spent family vacations "burying the beebee" (using every breeze to the fullest) out on Lake Michigan.

John was a Christian whose worldview anchored everything he did to making his world more like heaven. He applied this principle to his home life, work, leisure time, and church activities. John loved his church family and had a passion for people who needed to know Jesus as Lord.

John was elected to be a deacon in his church. He was excited about this calling and eager to contribute and provide some leadership. John served his first year learning the ropes. In his second year he became vice-chair; in his third and final year he served as chair.

John applied himself with vigor and joy to whatever he did—even the difficult things. He was definitely not a quitter; by nature, he was a leader and a problem solver. So it was uncharacteristic of John not to feel successful or positive about his involvement as a deacon. Before his three years of service were completed, he eagerly awaited the end of his term. He would be reluctant to serve again as deacon. What had gone wrong? What had sapped his enthusiasm and energy for this work?

Carol was a grade school teacher. She was conscientious in preparing her daily lesson plans. It was important to Carol to develop her teaching skills and to build strong professional relationships with her coworkers. Her concern for her students led her to interact with them and their parents outside of class.

Carol was married and had two children. She was devoted to her husband and eager to see her children develop their skills and interests through positive life experiences. Her son was in middle school and her daughter in high school. Church activities, music lessons, and sports dominated their schedules. Carol was busy!

She was also a devoted Christian. Carol had served on the mission committee, taught church school, and led a variety of other church activities. Her election as a deacon surprised nobody. She had a reputation for a compassionate heart and a knack for getting things done.

Carol found her deacon's work demanding—one more set of responsibilities on top of everything else. Yet it was also fulfilling and brought her joy and spiritual growth. What was the source of her high morale and satisfaction?

The difference between John's and Carol's experiences raise some questions about the best methods for building enthusiasm and a sense of fulfillment in deacons. The following suggestions may be helpful:

1. Experiencing spiritual growth and renewal through their service will significantly increase deacons' morale and satisfaction in service.

- *Devotions:* Devotions in John's council and diaconate meetings were often perfunctory. The council and diaconate assigned each member a date to choose a passage and pray. Unfortunately, that method disregarded each member's ability and interest in leading devotions.

Pastoral staff and the chairman of deacons crafted devotions in Carol's council and diaconate meetings. Her deacons meetings opened with half an hour of devotional time and discussion. Carefully chosen passages reflected Christ's mercy and focused on his call to Christians and his church to be merciful. These texts set a tone and expectation for the work of mercy. A guided discussion and thoughtful questions encouraged deacons to apply the Word to their own lives and to their work as deacons. These discussions encouraged Carol to connect her spiritual journey and diaconal experiences with the Holy Spirit's active intervention in life and helped her understand God in new ways. Carol began to walk and talk more with God.

A beginning list of passages for consideration is included in Appendix A.

- *Debriefing:* Debriefing, a form of guided discussion, helps connect deacons' spiritual journeys to stories or events shaped by God's incredible mercy. Carol's diaconate encouraged her to relate her ministry stories to other deacons. Sometimes she shared her frustration with the lack of congregational response to her requests for help. More often she told of needy people who were taking courageous steps forward. She gave accounts of members who were being changed through serving Jesus and their needy neighbors. Carol was consistently challenged to watch for God's divine intervention—for miracles in her life and in her "clients'" lives, and for God's movement in the hearts of his people.

- *Prayer:* Carol's diaconate consistently spent the final portion of each meeting in communal prayer. The deacons praised God for his work in their own lives, in the lives of those they served, and in their congregation. They pleaded with God for his intervention in situations where need was strong. Carol's diaconate knew that their work was God's work; they were merely his instruments. They waited expectantly for him to answer their prayers and held him to his promise to do far more through them than they could even imagine. Carol's prayer life blossomed.

2. Holding out a biblically informed vision of the office and the work expect-

ed from deacons will significantly increase deacons' morale and satisfaction in service.

John's orientation to office when he was first elected consisted of two components.

- At a council retreat, the pastor led a helpful Bible study examining the qualities and qualifications of office-bearers. The retreat included recreation time as well as guided discussion of issues currently facing the congregation. Elder and deacon district teams met to plan future visits.

- The first deacons meeting was spent teaching new deacons the procedures of how offerings were scheduled, collected, and counted.

John's vision of diaconal work developed from watching what the deacons did. This system of orientation for new deacons maintains yesterday's vision and system of ministry and does not challenge a deacon for the ministries of tomorrow. John simply settled into an unfulfilling routine.

Carol's orientation was similar to John's, except that an additional block of time was allowed for group study and reflection on the following:

- Church order articles that cast a vision for mercy ministries at the congregational and community levels of service, the regional and classis levels of service, and the national/international levels of service.

- The ordination form, which calls deacons to lead and develop the congregation's mercy ministry through offerings of wealth, time, and ability.

- The results of a recently completed community-needs assessment. This research clarified gaps in the existing social service network and inspired several ideas for new target and side-door ministries they should consider launching, among them a daycare ministry, a transportation ministry, and a car-repair ministry.

- The deacons' accomplishments during the preceding year and their goals and organizational changes to be implemented this year in order to increase ministry results.

By the end of her orientation, Carol knew the church was relying on her to develop ministries of mercy. She understood that she was to encourage the compassionate service of many members by calling them into ministry opportunities. She recognized that each deacon's contribution complemented the others' so that the church would be a beacon of reconciliation in the community.

3. Laying out clear goals and objectives and concrete ministry assignments can unleash deacons and significantly increase their morale and satisfaction in service.

Both John and Carol were aware of and appreciated the increased cultural expectation for improving performance in work arenas. Focusing on improved performance taught them greater effectiveness and efficiency. They were eager to grow in skill and knowledge; they wanted to make a difference.

John's deacons meetings and work were routine. They did "the count." The same few volunteers ran the food pantry. They made and approved the offering schedule. They reported on widow visits and on the four active benevolence cases. The routine was so well oiled that it practically ran itself. John often wondered if anyone would miss him should he just not show up at a meeting.

Carol was recruited to a specific diaconal assignment: she served as a contact person for a local clearinghouse organization that referred needy people to churches. She was told that she could realistically build this area of ministry to help ten or more families in the coming year. Many of them would be single-parent families who needed monthly support with paper products and items they could not purchase with food stamps. She learned how to develop contracts with interested families to help them plan for and achieve self-sufficiency with some church support.

Carol met and exceeded her goal of serving ten families. In each case, she trained a volunteer to be a support person to the needy family and helped volunteers develop contracts. She encouraged the volunteers and supported them in discipling their new friends. Carol began a support group for members involved in these ministries, which provided them an opportunity to hear each other's stories and to learn from one another. Carol achieved a deep sense of accomplishment in developing her ministry. She had made a difference for needy people, for church members as ministers, and in the church's outreach ministry in the community.

4. Attending to deacons personally can significantly increase their morale and satisfaction in service.

On several occasions, John did not know where to turn for leadership and di-rection, especially with several long-term cases involving chronic dependence on the diaconate. At the end of his term, he knew little more about helping people than when he began, and he felt let down by the church leaders for not providing more direction and support.

John also questioned certain tasks. He had to meet with the fellowship committee every month. His council's policy dictated that every member be appointed to one of the standing committees of the church as a council liaison. To John, this conveyed lack of trust. He thought this wasted his time and duplicated other efforts. But to whom could he convey these thoughts? Was he just being a rebel deacon? He decided not to rock the boat.

He wondered if church leaders respected him and his leadership. While he had good relationships with every council member, he didn't feel cared for or successful as a person. John speculated that others might feel the same way, but he hesitated to bring up these issues—no one else did.

Carol filled out a questionnaire, similar to the following, each month:

- What problems, issues, or barriers did you face this month in your diaconal ministry?

- What recommendations would you like to bring to the diaconate for consideration?

- What training, education, or resources would help you or your volunteers increase your effectiveness in service?

- What is your morale this month as a deacon?

Poor   Fair   Excellent

Either the chairperson of the diaconate or a pastoral staff person would respond to Carol's comments and questions. Within the week, she could expect a call. They cared about her. They wanted her to succeed and worked hard to assist her. Her support team was both a comfort and a resource.

Two: Defining the Work—Aligning the Workers

Peter loved serving as a deacon in his large suburban congregation. He drew a strong sense of holy pride from working with a diaconal team that helped so many needy people. His diaconate had assisted over a hundred families in the past year, including people who had experienced childhood sexual abuse; those with a variety of physical, psychological and emotional disabilities; and individuals struggling with addictions. They served grieving persons, the homeless, and seniors from both the church and community. Peter was honored to be part of this ministry team. He had never before considered himself a leader—he was a mechanic, a nuts-and-bolts kind of a guy, not a ministry leader.

Peter's joy in belonging to this ministry team mingled with his satisfaction in his own leadership niche as a deacon. For the first time in his adult life, Peter was doing lasting, important work in the church. This sense of mission gave him the extra energy needed for making late-night calls, attending additional meetings, and occasionally facing some rather unpleasant people.

Peter led his congregation's transportation ministry. His volunteer crew, which varied from seventeen to twenty-five members, helped low-income families do basic maintenance on their vehicles one weekend each month. In one year, they helped fourteen families find or keep permanent jobs by providing them with solid transportation.

Peter assigned volunteer mentors to each of these families. At weekly meetings, the mentors collected modest car payments and monitored other contract items negotiated in the recipients' ministry contracts. Car payments went to a revolving loan fund used for car purchase and repairs.

Peter immensely enjoyed the young people who participated in the car maintenance work. They were learning some important basic skills while serving others. As they worked together, he and the young volunteers would engage in soul-searching, growth-producing discussions. He would go home singing!

Susan served as a deacon in a small church in an older part of the city. She was surprised to be elected, but doing her best and fitting in turned out not to be difficult. She soon realized that besides collecting and counting the offerings, visiting some shut-ins, and occasionally responding to a member's request for financial aid, little else was expected. The monthly round of meetings were hectic—council meetings one night per month, deacons meetings another night per month, and education committee meetings yet another night. She attended the education committee meetings as the council's liaison. She also participated in the usual holiday basket deliveries to "special people" in the congregation. Susan figured she had to give up an average of one night per week.

Susan found two things difficult to handle. The first was the incessant demand for more money. Her congregation had lost so many giving families over the years that raising the budget had become an annual nightmare. Some in the congregation were low givers, but wasn't that to be expected? Most families seemed to give what they could. Adding to the financial pressure, three new families had moved to this lower-income community and asked for tuition assistance. Finances seemed to dominate most of the discussions at deacons meetings. They never found real solutions to the perpetual budget woes. Susan had a hard time sleeping after these long meetings.

The second difficult situation for Susan involved the discussion about a family the church had been helping for fourteen years. She soon discovered that the deacons discussed this family at almost every meeting. Their deacon contact always brought a report and another request for benevolent aid. Their needs included car repairs, unpaid heat bills, phone shut-off warnings, constant medical crises, work layoffs, and more. Susan believed that the benevolence money spent on this family did little good; the time spent discussing the case produced few results. She also disapproved of the patronizing and sometimes rude way the deacons talked about this family.

By her second year of service, Susan did most of the ministering to the elderly. The other deacons were younger men with budding careers, busy families, and few daytime hours to spare. Susan found joy in visiting the older members and hearing their testimonies. Her little effort produced a lot of thanks and goodwill. She resolved to make this her contribution to the diaconate and let the others handle the funds and the high-need cases. The other deacons seemed grateful not to have to visit all of their assigned shut-ins, so Susan endured the meetings and ministered to the elderly.

Peter's and Susan's diaconates operated differently and obtained different results. Among the differences were the following:

1. Defining the Vision

Susan's diaconate emulated the ministry and structures of the past. Peter's diaconate used to resemble Susan's, but began to change when in their devotional times they studied the calling of deacons. They became convinced that they had lost the heart of deaconing. They were transformed by a new vision for deacons—the understanding that God called them to the single purpose of building a merciful congregation who spent time, energy, and possessions to help poor and needy people experience his grace and hear his message of salvation.

2. Defining the Work

In Susan's diaconate, some tasks were clearly defined: the routine maintenance tasks of visiting the elderly, counting the collections, setting the offering schedules, and responding to members who asked for benevolent assistance. Each deacon was assigned to a standing committee of the church as a council liaison. Some deacons focused on tasks that fit their skills and passions, but the deacons equally shared all the jobs. They were programmed to reproduce the ministries and activities of last year and the year before that—yesterday's programs.

In their evaluation and planning process, Peter's diaconate discovered that too many deacons filled roles that did not produce ministry results. They also realized that some of their work did not properly fit their vision. His diaconate narrowed their focus to develop ministries of mercy, and within that focus concentrated on four key strategies for helping needy people.

- Forming **target ministries** (paper products ministry, refugee ministry, abuse ministry, homeless ministry, employment ministry, budgeting ministry, transportation ministry).

- Forming **recovery ministries** (Twelve-step recovery groups—AA, NA, Overeaters, Overspenders, divorce recovery groups).

- Forming **one-to-one ministry linkages** in which church members are paired with needy families for support and assistance in following mutually arranged plans to accomplish their dreams.

- Forming **next-step groups** to bring together needy individuals and families who share a desire to help one another accomplish their dreams. These groups provide support, self-help networking, accountability, and Bible study. On occasion they also engage in cooperative income-generating and cost-saving activities and pooled-income ventures.

Peter's diaconate retained responsibility for congregational stewardship. Three key functions were considered necessary to meet this responsibility.

- Evaluating organizations requesting financial support and setting offering schedules.

- Overseeing the collections of members' tithes and offerings and promoting faithful giving. The deacon who served as a member of the church finance committee performed this function.

- Conducting regular small group classes for people (members and community) desiring to regain control of their personal finances.

When Peter's diaconate faced the job of assigning workers, they began by evaluating the current work, asking what should be retained and who was best gifted to do each particular task. They then identified specific ministries that would change their community. They chose several, more than they could accomplish. Nine deacons were assigned to specific jobs. Because they were not the right people for the remaining jobs, three deacons resigned with no regrets. The diaconate then recruited people for six additional functions based on skills and passion for the work. Following this reorganization, Peter's diaconate was composed of one person for each of the following functions or ministries:

- *Chairperson*

  In addition to setting agendas, chairing the meetings and reporting on the diaconate's work to the congregation, the chairperson supervised each deacon in his or her functional assignment, offering encouragement, support, and new ideas.

- *Secretary*

  Along with the usual tasks of correspondence and taking minutes, the secretary reviewed organizations requesting offerings and set offering schedules.

- *Finance committee representative*

  In addition to working with the committee on budgeting and overseeing income and expenses, the finance deacon also supervised the counting committee and weekly collectors.

- *Regaining financial control*

  This deacon developed and conducted stewardship classes to teach people biblical principles for handling their funds. Small groups worked well to create accountability for change.

- Abuse ministry

- Refugee ministry

- Transportation ministry

- World hunger/social justice education and advocacy

- Ministry to elderly

- Regional projects

  This person represented the congregation on the regional denominational deacons committee.

- Ministry to people with disabilities

- Twelve-step groups and next-step groups

- Ministry to homeless

- Paper products ministry

  This was a ministry to aid low-income single parents.

- Grief ministry

3. Choosing the Workers— Recruitment of Deacons and Terms of Office

Workers who understand the vision, have a personal sense of urgency about it, and

are talented, trained, and supervised, will advance the work.

Susan's diaconate had no clear vision, nor did they work with urgency. New deacons were not particularly gifted, trained, or supervised for their duties. Most worked out of a sense of obligation rather than a desire to serve.

As deacons retired, Susan's church presented to their congregation the need for new deacons to fill these positions. They invited church members to nominate candidates, but few names were ever brought forward. As a result, the council usually devoted an evening to paging through the directory and listing names of eligible people. Anyone not ruled out by virtue of immoral behavior, work conflicts, or other obvious problems was considered eligible. The council then selected their candidates from the composite list and sent all nominees a letter informing them that their names would be on the ballot unless they appeared before the council on a set date to have their name removed. The deacons' names were always chosen after the elders' list was finalized. This church operated under the opinion that almost anyone could serve well as a deacon and that deacons' work was less important than elders' work.

In Susan's church, finding people willing to be nominated for office became increasingly difficult. They even changed from three-year to two-year terms in an effort to accommodate those who were unwilling to commit for so long.

By contrast, Peter's church discovered a new way to elect deacons. This method sustained the ministry momentum with strong leadership and developed continuity over time. They devised a simple application process that encouraged members with specific gifts to apply for specific diaconal roles. Other members could also nominate people for these roles. The council informed the congregation about functions or positions that needed new deacons and briefly described the work involved. The process remained open until enough people expressed interest in the work. The council screened applicants and nominees based on their talents, passion for service, and spiritual qualifications for church leadership. Finally, the congregation voted on the two best people.

The council also approved successive terms of service for leaders who were willing to continue their service, finding great joy in their service, achieving results in their ministries, and growing in their expertise as leaders.

Three: **Developing Vision**

Jim attended an educational conference for deacons, where he took part in workshops such as *Effective Ministry to Seniors, How to Increase Giving in the Congregation, How to Resettle a Refugee Family* and *How to Begin a Twelve-Step (Recovery) Program.* The day excited and inspired him. Traveling home, Jim asked his two fellow deacons which presentations they had attended. They listed workshop such as *Racial Reconciliation, Ministry to Homeless Families, Partnering with Nonprofits to Get Results, The Role of Deacon, Developing a Justice Ministry, The Role of Prayer for Ministry Leaders, Teaching Personal Stewardship* and *Developing a Congregational Disability Ministry.* More workshops were offered than they could attend.

The diversity of topics surprised all three deacons. Their diaconate basically collected and counted money, visited elderly members of the congregation, and gave benevolent aid to church families in crisis. They occasionally collected relief supplies for a local food and clothing distribution organization. But they did not consider themselves ministry developers; none of them had thought about deacons starting and supporting target and side-door ministries. (Both target and side-door ministries, by definition, attract unchurched people to the church or to church activities. Target ministries include a deliberate discipleship or evangelism component; side-door ministries simply create a flow of unchurched people to church-based activities.) They were amazed at how much some diaconates accomplished.

Jim commented that changing the way their diaconate functioned would require enormous effort. The others agreed and wondered whether it was worth the effort. Two of them were beginning the last year of their terms of service; how could they make so much change in one year? Four other deacons were not even interested enough to attend the conference. By the time they arrived home, Jim and the other two were ambivalent about introducing ideas or sharing their experience; the obstacles to change seemed too great.

During the next year, Jim became more spiritually restless about his own work as a deacon and about his diaconate's performance. He envisioned his church members responding to refugees, developing a latch-key ministry, working with low-income single parents, running abuse-recovery groups, and more. But none of this would happen unless the deacons developed a shared vision.

Defining the Vision

Jim and the other members of his diaconate began by talking about what vision is and how they should go about defining and refining their vision. They listed the following characteristics of vision:

- Vision is a mental, customized portrait of a preferable future that requires change.

- Vision affirms and learns from the past, recognizes the limitations and opportunities of the present, and pushes toward what could be in the future.

- Vision is a gift imparted by God to those who seek it through study and exercise of the spiritual disciplines (praying, fasting, journaling, meditating).

- Vision is based on an accurate understanding in three areas:

  — Who God is and what he wants.

  — Who you are and the role God has called you to fill.

  — Your ministry circumstances—both your congregation's gifts and interests and your congregation's and community's needs.

No two diaconates should have identical vision statements. Each congregation's history, current ministry environment, and opportunities for ministry are unique.

According to Barna Research, only 2 percent of churches have a vision statement. Even fewer diaconates do. Most churches duplicate yesterday; ministry styles, programs, and organization are simply rerun each year. Few church leaders spend time prayerfully discerning and discussing what God wants them to accomplish in the future.

So how can Jim help his diaconate capture God's preferred future for them?

Jim must begin by coming to terms with himself.

Is he willing to provide some leadership? Is he motivated appropriately—does he want change for God's sake or for his own reward? Is he able and willing to spend extra time to build a consensus around a new vision? Has he done preliminary work to be sure of where he is leading the diaconate? Are matters right in the rest of his life (with his spouse, his children, in his workplace) so that God can bless these efforts?

Jim has to be sure that his budding vision is from God.

Is it biblically consistent, and can he support his vision with Scripture? Has Jim prayed for both confirmation of the vision and guidance for each next step? Is he willing to be led by the Spirit? Has Jim applied any of the spiritual disciplines to his sense of God leading in this vision development? Has the Spirit confirmed this vision to him in any concrete or observable ways? Can Jim point to any signs or spiritual interventions in which God seemed to be confirming the vision?

Jim needs to know his ministry environment.

Can he depend on pastoral support? Will other deacons support his ideas? Initiating new ideas with as much support as possible from colleagues is always preferable.

Does he have a good handle on community needs based on an initial community survey or needs assessment? Vision is easier to promote if concrete ministry ideas can be produced from factual community demographics and information about needs.

Does Jim know what other churches and organizations in the community are doing? Duplicating vision is neither helpful or necessary; it creates competition rather than need-based ministry.

Does Jim have a clear grasp of the congregation's history of support for various types of diaconal ministry? Is his vision consistent and compatible with that history? Is his vision built on realistic congregational resources such as volunteerism, giving capacity, and available facilities? Does Jim have a clear sense of possible opposition to his vision? Is it realistic to overcome those barriers or points of opposition?

Has Jim sought wise counsel? Has he shared his ideas with mentors, spiritual leaders, accountability groups, or church leaders and received their support?

Jim, with support from all possible ministry leaders, invites the diaconate to begin a revisioning process.

This process can occur in a variety of settings. The most common are the following:

- In bits and pieces at successive deacons meetings over a period of several months.

- In a single deacons retreat.

- In two or three successive regular deacons meetings devoted to this process.

Jim's Agenda for Setting a Vision

1. Jim led opening devotions and prayer for the clear leading of the Holy Spirit and submission to his will.

2. Jim shared his story about how God had been leading him to the point of this meeting.

3. Jim selected Scripture passages for deacons to study in two small groups. (See Appendix A for a selection of Bible passages.) The full diaconate then discussed what God had revealed to them through those verses.

4. Jim assigned each deacon a document to study. Each was asked to report on it later to the whole diaconate.

- Church Order (Appendix B)

- Ordination Form (Appendix C)

- Synodical Reports (Appendix D)

- Types of Diaconal Ministry (Appendix E)

- Concentric Circles of Service (Appendix F)

5. Jim led a review of their accomplishments as deacons during the last five years.

   How many members had been involved with the deacons in ministries of mercy? How many people had been helped? How many target and side-door ministries had been added to meet people's needs? How many of those helped had actually accomplished their stated personal goals?

   Together they evaluated whether God was pleased with those results. They also discussed their own level of satisfaction.

6. Jim shared the results of a preliminary needs assessment he had completed from the church and community. (See Appendix G.)

7. Jim led a short presentation on "What is a vision statement?"

8. Jim again led in a prayer for clarity of vision.

9. Jim asked each participant to draft a vision statement that meets the criteria of Appendix H.

10. Jim paired participants to combine and refine a single vision statement from their two respective statements.

11. They repeated the process in groups of four deacons.

12. Jim assigned one deacon (this could be a small group of three) to forge all drafts into a single draft statement for the entire diaconate.

13. Jim closed the process with prayers of thanksgiving.

14. Jim circulated the new draft and allowed additional input until the next deacons meeting. The diaconate then approved their final vision statement.

Four: **Accountability, Support, and Feedback**

Doug was a deacon in his late thirties. By his own confession, he had wasted his teens and twenties on self-indulgent pleasures and thrills. He was eager to establish himself in the business world and used his college business degree to land himself a fairly lucrative position. He was aggressive and successful, as was his company, which recognized and appreciated Doug's contributions. His influence and benefits grew incrementally over time.

During the first ten years of his business career he married and had two daughters. Doug is not exactly sure how, but during those years God weaned him from the lure of thrills and success. In his heart he became a servant. Satisfying customers and spending time with his family motivated him most. He actively followed Jesus and willingly worked in the church.

When Doug was elected to be an administrative deacon, he observed that attitudes toward performance in the church differed from those in the marketplace.

First, people in the business world, while having a diverse set of personal motivations, were all similarly focused and committed to a common set of goals. In the marketplace, feedback systems rigorously measured inputs, outputs, and results. Most people were willing and eager to be part of a team that built on one another's energies and contributions. Teamwork contributed to individual and corporate success. The marketplace defined, stated, and measured that success.

In the church, Doug found that defining success was elusive. People fought new direction and rarely developed common goals. At best, people agreed about types or categories of ministry such as education, worship, service, missions, and fellowship. They also reached some consensus on preservation of individual programs.

Defining a vision and establishing measurable goals seemed out of reach. Performance issues, if they were raised, focused on busyness of staff and members. The need to meet congregational budgets overshadowed other goals. Nothing remotely resembling results-focused goals or performance was ever mentioned during his term of service.

Second, the marketplace paid attention to processes used to produce results and recognized that the human systems used and the technologies employed also influenced results. Business leaders constantly evaluated more efficient ways to use their staff. They were quick to send staff for additional training and skill development to keep them on the cutting edge. They willingly provided training and capital for new technology if it would increase performance while being cost-effective. Doug often attended business seminars and conventions. He learned new computer software applications and become familiar with car phones and fax machines.

But Doug's experience in the church was far different. He underwent no diaconal orientation or training until his classis sponsored an event during his third year of service. Although Doug was responsible for recruiting volunteers to count offerings, no inventory system of members' gifts or interests was available to him as reference. Nobody had considered improved methods; in fact, the counting and recording systems had not changed in over twenty years. Deacons were elected without regard for their skills or interests in ministries of mercy. People were selected to fill slots rather than deployed based on gifts, interests, passions, and capacities for levels of service.

The decision-making process in the church was a leftover from the past. Too many people were involved in decisions, which had to pass through too many organizational layers before implementation. The mechanics of making decisions stifled any effort at change. The current system did not entrust capable people with both responsibility and authority.

He recalled a time when their church needed a new copy machine: Two deacons spent six hours each doing initial research because neither knew anything about copy machines. Next, nine deacons spent two hours considering machine specifications and their budget ramifications. Then the whole council of nineteen people spent three hours making the final decision. In conclusion, they decided to delay purchase for six months. They spent approximately ninety hours of leadership time deciding to wait six months for a machine that had marginal value to ministry results. Doug wondered what would have happened if forty-five of those leadership hours had been allocated to neighborhood outreach, serving single-parent families, or resettling a refugee family.

The church was also slow to invest in technology and support services and did not yet own a computer or a fax machine. The church secretary worked only twelve hours per week, too few to be marginally helpful. How could they be a ministering organization reaching people and serving the community? Doug surmised accurately that these must not be his church's goals.

Third, business people expected changing environments and markets that were constantly fluctuating. The marketplace anticipated changes in processes and technologies in order to keep pace; they knew the rate of that change was rapidly increasing.

Doug could find few feedback systems in the church except for attendance figures for worship, committee meetings, and Wednesday evening programs. Finding people to fill positions concerned them all, but no one thought about whether recruits were interested in or skilled for those positions. No one asked whether those positions contributed to ministry goals; everyone assumed that the way they had always organized themselves for ministry was the only way. They never discussed alternative organization methods or systems issues.

The longer Doug was involved in his diaconal duties, the more out of place he felt. He felt as though he had to enter a time warp whenever he did church work. Worse, he received little sympathy or understanding when he raised these issues in the diaconate or council. The church culture wanted to leave the systems and technologies in the marketplace and keep them out of the church. Change and innovation were not welcome.

Accountability = Support + Feedback

Like most deacons, Doug wants something from his term of service. He may have been unable to articulate it when first elected, but he knows that if he hasn't gotten that something by the end of his term of service, he will not agree to serve again. He wants to grow spiritually through his service, and he wants to make a difference. What can a church do to help Doug attain these two goals?

- *Recognize that Doug is on a spiritual journey.* He wants to be a growing, serving Christian who sees God more clearly, understands him more fully, and lives for him more faithfully. Doug needs a Spirit-filled leader (probably the chairperson of the diaconate or an involved pastor) to help him reflect and grow in his relationship to God through this time of service. Crafting devotional times and investing personal time to help Doug reflect on his spiritual growth are the best ways to energize him for his work.

- *Realize that Doug has never been a deacon before.* His only public view of deacons' work is seeing them pass a collection plate at worship. He also knows they are to care for the poor, but he doesn't know how. He needs and wants high quality orientation and training to help him understand his role. If he doesn't get it, Doug will watch carefully what other deacons do and reproduce yesterday's activities. If he does get it, he will use his time and talents accordingly.

- *Discover Doug's gifts and passions and assign him a particular function in the diaconate that builds on these skills.*

- *Ask Doug each month what problems, barriers, or frustrations he experienced* so that the leaders can help him minimize the negative aspects of his work.

- *Ask Doug each month what education or assistance he needs to do the job.* Give him access to resources that build his competence and increase his performance.

- *Ask Doug each month to bring carefully thought-out recommendations to the diaconate.* Doug's experience can be used to increase effectiveness in ministry. Doug's workplace background can help his church take next steps in ministry.

- *Ask Doug each month how he feels about his service.* If his morale is low, find out why and help him resolve any difficulties. If his morale is high, encourage him to share his story to encourage the other deacons and church members. Most high morale is related to ministry accomplishments or seeing God perform signs and wonders through people like Doug. These are important stories to tell.

- *Ask Doug each month what he accomplished, whom he served, and what the outcomes of that service were.* These performance questions will help Doug stay focused on his task and will convey to him the responsibility and accountability entrusted to him. Since his is a voluntary position, Doug could too easily let the work slide in lieu of other demands. Regular accountability will help him examine his priorities and encourage him to think about effectiveness and efficiency issues.

A sample monthly questionnaire for deacons is found in Appendix I. Deacons who use this kind of questionnaire to report to one another quickly build a sense of mutual accountability for performance and results. This tool also gathers stories to tell to the congregation about how God is using them to extend his mercy in the church and community.

People today expect performance from their institutions. The church is no exception. Volunteers such as deacons will not serve out of obligation; however, they will gladly serve and make enormous contributions of time, talent, and resources if they are fully supported, equipped, and accountable for service.

Single-Line Accountability

Doug, like all other volunteers in the church, needs and deserves one person who accepts responsibility to help him grow in his assignment for the sake of his morale and spiritual development. The church needs Doug to perform to the best of his ability for the sake of the church. The church will thrive when her members enthusiastically contribute to her vision and goals. If Doug does not perform to capacity in his assigned area, the church loses ground. Developing an accountability system that helps Doug flourish is in everybody's best interest.

The least complicated and most direct organizational system to provide this kind of support is a single-line accountability system. Each person in the organization reports to only one person for his or her performance and support. Doug would likely report to the chairperson of the diaconate. The chairperson would likely report to a staff person or senior pastor. If Doug would recruit seven or eight people to serve under him in diaconal work, then he would be responsible for their performance and growth.

Authority and Responsibility

Allocating to frontline workers the authority necessary to design and implement their work is critical to the success of volunteer organizations. Doug is given responsibility for collecting and counting offerings using volunteers. If he is told to do it a certain way, in a certain place, and at a certain time following an established process, Doug will feel that the church wants him to be a robot that performs a predetermined function. He may be obedient for a while, but he will not be fulfilled. If, on the other hand, Doug is allowed to use his energy, creativity, and knowledge of financial systems to collect, count, and record the offerings, he can be a blessing by creating the simplest, most reliable system he can think of. He will feel good about his contribution if he improves on the previous system. The same holds true with any function or task area in the church. Volunteers will be most fulfilled when they are unleashed to use their God-given talents and creativity to accomplish the defined tasks.

A regular accountability system, such as the one in Appendix I, will help deacons hold each other responsible to increase their effectiveness and efficiency over time. Regular reports to the chairperson will provide plenty of built-in restraint to manage potential problems. Meanwhile each deacon enjoys full freedom to use his or her gifts and produce results. Nothing energizes them more.

Five: **Helping More People**

The Christian Reformed Church has two primary documents for defining the work of deacons. They are the *Ordination Form for Deacons* and the relevant articles of the denomination's *Church Order*. After studying these documents, deacons have concluded that the following results are likely if deacons are faithful to their calling and if God is blessing their labors.

1. *More Christians will serve needy people.* Donations of time and talent and material offerings will increase to help poor and needy people.

2. *More needy people will receive help.* Deacons will find needy people to help both within the congregation and the community.

3. *Many of those helped will solve their disabling problems and attain new levels of self-sufficiency.* An increasing percentage of aid and volunteerism will be directed at helping people take next steps in their lives rather than just putting bandages on the same old problems.

4. *More funds will be allocated to poor people.* Education in stewardship, effective ministry programs, and personal involvement of members in ministry often result in reallocation of discretionary income to ministry from consumptive alternatives.

5. *More people will become church members.* Christian mercy combines effective programming, timely and carefully directed aid, and gospel witness to recipients. When these are offered in the context of long-term, loving relationships in which Christians authenticate the gospel witness, recipients are often irresistibly drawn toward Christ and his church.

(*Note: CRWRC and several diaconal conferences are using these criteria for evaluating effectiveness in their work with deacons.*)

One of the paradoxes of Christianity is that believers on the one hand reach out to worldly people to introduce them to Christ, and on the other hand disassociate from them. Many church members cannot name one unchurched friend with whom they interact frequently. Many cannot even name one poor and needy acquaintance. This isolation has too often resulted in a lack of understanding and compassion for people who are different. Many congregations are segregated from the very community God calls them to serve.

Another paradox is that people who become faithful disciples of God tend to rise above their poverty and pain. They make different choices, adopt Christian principles of lifestyle stewardship, and experience the blessings of a community that shares wealth, time, talents, and opportunities. They work together to bless each other through education and shared learning. The paradox is that while God gives good gifts to Christians, he calls them to use those gifts to care for the poor, the alien, the needy widow, and the dispossessed. Blessings are given to be given away. They are meant for kingdom building, not personal consumption.

Unfortunately, Christians often live in isolation from poor people. Too many Christians have become consumers of God's gifts of discretionary time, talents, and resources. They have turned his gifts into personal assets and cut themselves off from opportunities to be his blessing to others.

Many poor and needy people want and need help. Government and social service organizations may provide survival goods, therapy, and skills training. But social workers will not open up their personal lives, relationships, and connections to opportunities that poor people need. That would violate professional distance. Christians must fill this gap; unconditional love, personal friendship, and shared opportunity produce in needy people the will to persist in achieving their goals. The Word of God best takes root in this environment.

Every Christian needs to be personally involved with unchurched and poor people because

- they belong to God.

- God calls Christians to witness to them.

- God calls Christians to serve others in times of pain and poverty.

- Christians need to share and serve lest they take their time, talents, and treasures too seriously and forget that these resources belong to God.

- God uses life journeys to teach us lessons in the value of community, the art of sharing, and the joy of celebrating. God often uses poor and unchurched

people to help Christians find different points of reference in life—they often draw Christians back to their self-sacrificing God.

Which ministry methods will help deacons achieve results in these areas? Deacon can consider several categories of diaconal programming.

One-to-One Referrals

By working with community agencies, deacons can generate a flow of poor and needy people who want and need Christians to partner with them in their journey toward wholeness. Agencies, fearing blatant proselytizing, may be reluctant at first to trust church members. But they realize their clients need love, acceptance, role models, and support people in order to overcome their problems and rise above poverty. Few other organizations besides the church offer true community to hurting people.

Three questions can encourage social service agencies to begin making referrals:

1. What are the unmet human needs of your clients?

2. Is anyone else offering to meet these needs? Why not let us?

3. Will you let your clients know we are willing to help, so they can refer themselves?

Deacons need to be honest with people referred. The church offers a long-term, supportive relationship with a caring, loving Christian. The church also uses limited amounts of aid to supplement the resources that people already have available to help them achieve their life goals. Aid that is not directed toward recipients' goals will only create dependency. Screening is essential to find those clients who have a dream and who are willing to first use their own resources to begin achieving that dream.

In recruiting church members to befriend and support poor and needy people, deacons must be honest with church members about their expectations. They expect the volunteers to

- pray daily for their new friend.

- spend a minimum of one hour per week with their new friend until God closes the door on the relationship. The new friend may be a friend for life.

- use their personal resources as God directs them to help their new friend. Aid is only helpful when it is directed toward a goal.

- work with the deacons in allocating benevolent aid effectively to help the recipient achieve his/her goals.

- share their faith, philosophy of life, and values at appropriate times with their friend.

Deacons can create a safe and structured environment for church volunteers by assessing the recipients' needs and working with them to create a contract or agreement that spells out their goals and the steps needed to achieve them.

How many referrals can a congregation handle? That number varies, but it is reasonable to link at least one out of every ten adult members in the congregation in a long-term relationship with a poor or needy family.

Here is one example of a referral that would never have happened if a relationship did not exist between the Department of Social Services and a diaconate:

Tanya was a single parent with a ten-year-old son and a fourteen-year-old daughter. Her ex-husband paid her minimal child support. She was unemployed and receiving food stamps, along with some general assistance funds. She had just remodeled an apartment before her partner of eight years left her and she lost her job. She had $13,000 in credit debt and was losing her car for lack of payments. She desperately needed some dental work done but had no insurance to pay for it. Carol, a deacon, received Tanya's name with some scant details about her needs from a Department of Social Services worker. Carol met with Tanya to analyze both her current needs and to discover Tanya's skills and dreams for the future. Within two meetings, they had worked out a long-term plan.

This is what the plan included:

1. The diaconate acting as guarantor for dental bills to correct the immediate problems so the dentist would proceed with the work. Tanya could pay the bill over two years.

2. An agreement for the diaconate to pay one dollar for every dollar that Tanya paid against her bills up to $600 over the next six months. Money would be paid to creditors after receipts were seen. The arrangement would be reviewed after six months.

3. The diaconate's help in securing a used car to get her to work and back. Tanya would pay the insurance, title fees, and operating expenses.

4. Leads to employment. Within three days, Tanya had found a job that paid nine dollars per hour.

5. Free child care provided by church members so that Tanya could attend

school two nights per week to work on her BA degree.

6. A plan to get more assistance from the children's father.

7. A commitment from Tanya to attend a small group budgeting class the church regularly held in twelve-week cycles.

The deacons recruited Jane, a church member, to be Tanya's personal friend and mentor during the anticipated two-year contract. Jane was excited to jump into the relationship. Her involvement contained structure, safety, and time limits. Tanya agreed to meet weekly with Jane for contract review and personal support.

Target Ministries

Target ministries are activities or group meetings built around the needs of members, but also involving nonmembers and unchurched people. Common target ministries include the following:

- A Christian childcare program.

- A Christian twelve-step recovery group.

- A ten-month seniors program.

- A support group for children who have lost parents through death or divorce.

- A marriage-enrichment seminar conducted by the church.

Target ministries are usually run by the church and are Christian in their orientation; they include a deliberate discipleship component. Although they are usually formed to meet the needs of members, nonmember participation is equally appropriate. When community residents participate, they can become a strong venue for evangelism, discipleship, and church growth. Through this kind of Christian programming, the church becomes a familiar and friendly place to nonmembers. Because long-term satisfying relationships frequently spring from these ministries, they become front-door activities resulting in church growth.

Side-Door Ministries

Side-door ministries resemble target ministries, except that they usually do not have an overt discipleship or evangelism component. They are simply activities the church hosts, often begun when a person approaches the church as a viable source of usable and available space, or when members request to use space for something they need.

Side-door ministries include many well-known programs:

- AA, NA, Al-Anon, Overeaters Anonymous, and other national programs rent space from a church.

- Head Start uses church facilities for a preschool program.

- A community agency operates a food pantry through the church.

- A crib ministry builds cribs and sets them up in people's homes.

Churches are finding creative ways to bring information about their worship and other ministries to people who participate in side-door activities. They are capitalizing on the flow of people to their facilities by inviting them to other church events and groups.

Deacons can use these activities as part of their portfolio of services available to needy people as well as use them to invite participants to receive additional help for other needs.

A growing number of churches are expanding the types and numbers of target and side-door ministries as a means to increase the flow of unchurched people to church facilities and members. They are becoming known as seven-day-a-week churches. There are several reasons for this growing trend:

- Increased use of facilities.

- More ways to meet members' needs.

- More ways to make the church a user-friendly place to people who would otherwise be unlikely to use it.

- More ways to invite people to find healing and help.

- More opportunities to evangelize and disciple people.

- More opportunities for the church to influence the culture and community.

- Opportunities and methods for churches to increase staff. Through fees for services, churches can add activities and staff without dramatically increasing the budget.

Deacons can significantly increase the number of people they help by adding to the number and variety of target and side-door ministries they make available to members and the community. For every target and side-door activity offered, several more people will be helped.

Only two factors limit the number of target and side-door ministries a church can offer.

1. *Leadership.* Are leaders available to develop and nurture the ministry?

2. *Facilities.* Is appropriate space available for the ministry?

Some examples of target and side-door ministries currently offered by Christian Reformed Churches in West Michigan are listed in Appendix J.

Next-Step Groups

How does a deacon or church do volunteer work with five families instead of one without becoming overwhelmed and burned out? They work with them together instead of individually.

Poor and needy people usually need one-on-one assistance from deacons (or people with training) to diagnose their situations and establish plans for change. But once the plan is established it is often powerful enough to bring these people into a group that meets regularly. They can share their plans and hold one another mutually accountable. The group can give members advice on how to amend behaviors and how to pursue alternative options; they can even share resources. When members experience unconditional love, honesty, and mutual support, their energy for change increases tremendously. With good leadership, these groups can assimilate new members for churches.

As with Alcoholics Anonymous and other dependency-alleviating programs, recipients can often call each other's bluffs, distinguish true efforts from faked efforts, and genuinely support one another. Small groups have a rare power to transform behavior through high accountability and shared commitment to one another's well-being. One group member trying to feign progress threatens the integrity of the entire group, so the other participants are quick to encourage honest change.

Many poor and needy people are able to get off public assistance. Without additional support, however, they seem to stop growing beyond this level of economic well-being. Next-step groups can serve individuals who graduate from substance abuse programs, individuals just released from prison, and individuals who are devastated by divorce and its sudden economic woes. Any family that is reaching for a new point of self-reliance and goal attainment is a prime candidate for a next-step group. By forming next-step groups, deacons can multiply the number of families they work with at any given time.

Jose and Maria were homeless. She was in a shelter with two children; he was in jail. Four years later, their family has grown to six. They are both working low-income jobs and they are barely squeaking by as proud first-time homeowners (via a land contract a church member helped them secure). They are still at high risk. Maria still yells at the kids a lot and displays signs of her unresolved abusive childhood. She has changed jobs three times in eighteen months without advancement. Jose continues to be a passive leader in the home. He bottles up his anger and frustration and disappears for hours at a time without consulting Maria. Their four young children are a handful, and neither parent has much energy to spend with them. Their marriage is rocky.

Jose and Maria will likely continue to struggle and probably fail without some kind of continuing support network. They need to face some of their fears, problems, and goals. The couple does not have one friend who accepts them as they are and loves them. They are ideal candidates for a next-step group where they can be loved, challenged, supported, chided, and grounded. They are open to spiritual renewal and discipleship. They don't attend a church regularly, but both talk openly of their need for God and their belief that he is the giver and sustainer of life.

Networking with Existing Organizations

A church in the core city of Holland, Michigan, recently began to face its membership decline seriously. The community was changing; new problems included gangs, muggings, gunshots, graffiti, and other signs of social ills. Church members were relocating and changing their church memberships. In another ten years, the doors of the church would close if they didn't aggressively and intentionally refocus their ministries to their neighborhood. They surveyed their community, looking for needs to fill and ways to make connections with community families.

They recognized that unattended youth were a problem. They began dreaming of a way to reach those kids and turn this community concern into a ministry strength. They formed a partnership with Boys and Girls Clubs of America. They fenced in their large parking lot and ran supervised summer and after-school basketball, boxing, hockey, and other sports. At the same time they added an alternative-style worship service that would be more seeker sensitive. This combination met the needs of the neighborhood. Without the initial partnership with the Boys and Girls Club of America, the church would not have had the funds or the personnel to make the necessary changes. The partnership gave new life.

Partnerships or networking with other organizations can help deacons

- discover new ministry ideas.

- build new capacity from under-utilized preexisting resources.

- prevent duplication of services.

- create a flow of people for ministry.

- bring otherwise inaccessible resources to members and the community.

- help the partner flourish by building spiritual roots and programming to the work.

Forming Christian Community Development Organizations

Madison Square Church in Grand Rapids, Michigan, is located in a decaying urban community. Housing is old, and much of it is in disrepair. Crime is high, and drug traffic is prolific; social problems abound. The deacons' primary concerns have been with member care and organizational and financial issues. They also cooperate with area emergency networks to aid needy people in the neighborhood.

Addressing root problems in the community was once beyond their vision and capacity, but they had a member with a vision and great skills for organizing and networking. They launched him into ministry by creating a new nonprofit Christian community development organization called Vinedresser to address urban issues and bring renewal to the community.

Vinedresser, in its first year of ministry, began a variety of programs:

- *Moms in Unity,* a support program for mothers

- *Young Dads,* a support program for seventeen- to twenty-five-year-old dads who were not actively involved with their children

- *Partnership with a Bird House Project,* to help homeless people have gainful employment and learn skills to eventually run their own business

- *Writers Workshop,* to help budding journalists develop marketable skills

- *Partnership with Jubilee Jobs,* to help prepare unemployed people for jobs and then match them with employment opportunities

- *Partnership with Family Talk,* a counseling service helping residents from the community

- *Creating a Work Force Preparation Model* with local businesses to train and employ local residents

Vinedresser is developing many program opportunities for community residents to help them turn their lives around. During the first nine months of their programming, they helped eighty-six people; sixty-two of them took significant steps towards self-sufficiency. Every participant in the Vinedresser programs is nurtured spiritually in groups or by Madison Square Church. Thirty-nine participants have been assimilated into a church or Bible study.

While Vinedresser is a separate, ecumenical organization, it is integrally connected to Madison Square Church. Two of the pastors are board members, and the church is committed to use the congregation to evangelizing and discipling Vinedresser participants. The partnership between them is organic, built around common values, ministry philosophy, and a strong relationship between church staff and Vinedresser staff.

Sometimes running ministry programs outside the organizational entity of the church is expedient. The danger in doing so is potential loss of evangelism, discipleship, and Christian nurture in programs. Another risk is losing a basic Christian philosophy of ministry that integrates social and spiritual change. Some parachurch organizations have become little more than social-service organizations in the name of ministry.

But the advantages are many.

1. *Organizational flexibility and freedom*

   • Freedom from restraints that exist in many congregations to run social ministries. Budgets, salaries, use of facilities, and other competing resources do not become points of contention or competition.

   • Freedom from church decision-making systems that can combat new ministry ideas and models.

2. *Access to revenues and grants that are not available to churches.* Some suburban churches, philanthropists, foundations, governments, and private donors will not give to churches but will give to nonprofit organizations (even those integrally connected to an anchor church).

3. *Freedom to incorporate in the leadership and design of programs participants who are not members of the church.* Churches often have membership and spiritual qualifications that need to be met for official roles in the ministry.

4. *Easier access to other local charities and social service organizations for cooperation in meeting recipients' needs.* Some agencies and charities are suspicious of working with churches but are willing to cooperate with other nonprofit organizations.

5. *Easier access to businesses and employers for a range of services.* Entrepreneurial leaders are often frustrated with churches' decision-making processes and time lines. Nonprofit organizations are often more responsive and flexible.

6. *Easier access to residents who may fear involvement with a church.*

7. *Access to a broader range of volunteers and donors.*

8. *Easier access to community organizations such as schools and public agencies who interpret their boundaries for participation in terms of sectarian affiliation.*

Churches that want to stand out as points of community revitalization, social witness, and justice may be able to do so better through integrated partnerships with separate nonprofit organizations.

Deacons need to address some basic questions:

• How will we find and assist more poor and needy people?

• How will we help them move toward problem-solving and goal attainment?

• How will we make it safe and manageable for busy people to volunteer their time, talents, and belongings with poor and needy people?

• How can we do all this while appropriately introducing them to Jesus, who is the way, the truth, and the life?

Six: **Working with Needy Families**

- In 1994, the average American wage earner spent in excess of four hundred dollars more than he or she earned.

- In 1994, total individual debt in the United States exceeded three trillion dollars.

- In 1994, 23 percent of the average household's take-home pay was committed to payment of existing debts (excluding home mortgages).

- In 1994, 56 percent of divorcees cited financial tension as a primary cause of their marital problems.

These are national statistics. Deviation from these numbers in churches is usually minimal. Not surprisingly, many church members struggle financially. Average American church attendees give little more than 2.5 percent of their income to charitable causes. Most deacons realize their churches contain many low givers and nongivers.

Churches that develop user-friendly methods of teaching biblical principles for faithful financial living to their members and community will literally save marriages and bring contentment to financially burdened families. This chapter will not teach the scriptural principles and their daily applications; these are available through several existing resources (see Appendix K). Instead this chapter will focus on values and principles for working with people who have financial needs.

Churches must keep five general rules in mind when working with financially needy people:

1. *Every family is different and needs to be treated with dignity and respect.* That means individual responses must be crafted for each family that needs help.

2. *People with financial needs are usually in pain.* Attending to them personally and identifying with their pain may be more important than dealing with financial solutions. People can live with pain and some financial discomfort; they struggle far more with loneliness, isolation, low esteem, and fear of calamity. Being a caring friend may be more important than solving financial problems. Using small groups in a church into which people can be channeled to experience unconditional love is one of the most important methods for sustaining people in crises.

3. *Giving financial aid to people in financial need always risks creating dependency.* Financial aid alone is rarely an adequate response to the need.

4. *The two primary solutions to financial need—decreasing spending, and increasing income—almost always require long-term relationships with high accountability in order for new behaviors to take root.*

5. *All of the resources of this world belong to God.* They are all at his dis-

posal and under his discretionary control. Intercessory prayer is our first and most important activity for bringing about change in every situation of financial need.

Working with Financially Needy Families in the Church

Financial needs lie deep in the body of Christ. The percentage of low givers and nongivers is ample testimony to this problem. But often the greatest need is a willingness and discipline to part with God's money. Many members have not learned that money, like their time, talents, and possessions, belongs to God. They also have not learned spiritual contentment.

Financially needy families within the church typically fall into one of four categories:

1. *An Emergency Need*

Bert just lost his job. His family income was around $50,000. Unfortunately, Bert and his family were carrying a credit debt load of $3,700 when he was fired without notice as part of a company restructuring process. Becky, his wife, was still recovering from a stroke, and insurance did not cover all of her therapy costs. They were contemplating taking a second mortgage on the house to pay the back bills and tide them over until Bert found new work.

How can deacons best respond to emergency needs like Bert and Becky's?

Show Bert and Becky your care and concern by **visiting them** as soon as you hear of his job loss. Inquire about their financial situation and ask them if they desire help of any kind. Pray with them. Express your love and commitment to help them through their crisis.

Enlist people to **pray for them daily** until they have new employment. This can be done anonymously. God wants us to pray and has promised to hear and respond to our prayers.

If Bert and Becky are part of a **small group** in the church, work with the group leader to make sure that someone is visiting them weekly during the time of crisis. Offer to use benevolent funds to support the small group as they find ways to respond to the family's needs. Channel aid, whenever possible, through the small group.

Arrange for **acts of kindness** from the congregation. Find someone to pay anonymously one month's education costs, a car payment, or a house payment; or ask five members to send them one hundred dollars anonymously during the next month.

If it is appropriate, **work out a plan** with Bert and Becky that keeps them from facing additional crises. Help them find freedom from financial stresses so that they have the psychological capacity to work hard at taking next steps in their lives. This can take the form of using benevolent aid to postpone payment on certain bills; finding employment opportunities for Bert to pursue, both temporary and permanent; helping them sort out and sell disposable assets; and finding them a budget counselor.

Encourage Bert and Becky to keep personal daily logs/diaries of events, feelings, and spiritual interventions during this time. This will help them stay aware of God at work in their lives. This can also help them share their pains and triumphs with other Christians. They can help other believers grow in their faith journeys by sharing what God is doing in their lives.

2. A Disability

Trent is a forty-two-year-old glass/window installer. He has three boys. His wife, Sue, works four days a week to supplement the family's income. Combined, their annual income approaches $45,000. Their eldest son is sixteen and has Down's Syndrome. Trent's annual Christian education bill is $17,000; they cannot pay it without assistance.

Mary is mentally ill; the official diagnosis is paranoid schizophrenia. Her mental illness surfaced and was diagnosed when she was in her late teens. At age fifty-seven, after two failed marriages and years of periodic institutionalization, she now lives in an adult foster care home. She began attending church regularly with her daughter two years ago and has asked to become a member. Federal and state aid programs meet her basic needs, but her discretionary income is less than thirty dollars per week. Her financial problems are compounded by her inability to make appropriate choices in her purchases.

How can deacons best respond to financial needs arising from disabilities?

Most adults like Mary with permanent disabilities have a financial guardian or legal payee to help them manage their finances. Deacons can **work out a plan with the payees** to give appropriate small gifts to increase their quality of life. *Note: Most adults with disabilities will experience a reduction in their allocation of aid if they receive additional income. "In-kind" donations are better than cash gifts.*

Far more important to the Marys of the world are people who will occasionally take them to breakfast or lunch and spend time being a friend. Mary loves being included at church picnics, going to the ladies softball games, and attending church social functions even though her ability to actively participate is limited. Mary will find a level of contentment living on a meager income if she also experiences the unconditional love and acceptance of a **small group** of members.

Churches must **develop systems of supplemental aid** to respond to needs like Trent's. They can include special offerings and appeals, Christian education endowment funds, and fund raisers. Deacons need to make sure that children with disabilities have the same access to spiritual and physical care and growth as any other children of the congregation.

As important as Christian education support for families like Trent's are the social support systems that **offer the parents times of respite.**

3. The Fixed-Income Elderly

Martha is seventy-three years old. Her husband, Tom, died seven years ago. Tom didn't believe in insurance, and he never invested for retirement. Martha rarely worked outside of the home. She has no income besides Social Security. Her monthly income was usually enough to meet her daily expenses, but her property taxes and any additional expenses were consistently beyond her reach.

How can deacons best respond to financially needy elderly?

Little can be done to increase Martha's income. Providing years of supplemental aid is not reasonable or good stewardship. But the church might find lower-cost housing for Martha in one of the following ways:

- The church could find lower-cost housing for her.

- A member or family could take her into their home.

- A church could help Martha link with another senior to reduce living costs and increase companionship.

- The deacons may want to help a group of seniors lease or purchase a home for older members where several seniors could live together under one roof.

- Martha may have enough resources from the equity in her home and her Social Security income to make a transition to an existing senior-housing facility in the community.

4. Financially Dependent Members

John was a third-generation church member. When he was young, John struggled in school. He dropped out by the time he was sixteen and floated from job to job. At age twenty-four he married, but he and his wife continued living at his parents' home. John and Tina had three children. John could never hold a job, but he was adamant that women should not work outside of the home, so Tina never did. They never had quite enough to get out on their own. When his father died, they inherited the house and began caring for John's aging mother.

Somehow John and Tina became dependent on the church for their financial problems. No one seems to know how or when it began, but at least every other month, John and Tina presented the deacons with another bill. The bills had to be paid; they couldn't live without electricity, or lose their house to back taxes, or drive their car without insurance. From the deacons' point of view, it would cost them more not pay the bills, which would trigger worse financial consequences if left unpaid. Over time

John and Tina forged a pattern of going from crisis to crisis with deacons bailing them out. That pattern continued for over thirteen years.

How can deacons best respond to financially dependent members?

People like John and Tina have subtly turned responsibility for their welfare over to the church. Change, though necessary, will likely be difficult and stormy. **Invite several people to pray for the deacons and John and Tina** during this time of change.

Visit John and Tina and **show them the total amount of money, as far back as it has been recorded, that has been allocated to their problems.** In John and Tina's case that amount exceeded $15,000. Point out that after $15,000 of aid, the underlying problems of inadequate income or misallocation of income have not changed. Let them know the deacons want to help them address the underlying problems so that they can become financially independent. They also have to understand that every dollar of aid they get is a dollar that someone else cannot receive. Inform them that the deacons can no longer pay their bills unless it is part of a mutually worked-out plan to help them increase their income or reallocate their income.

Work out a plan or contract with the family. (See Appendix L.)

Recruit a member to become their lay minister and take on certain responsibilities.

- Pray daily for them and love them.

- Visit them weekly to encourage them to follow their plan.

- Inform the deacons regularly about their progress.

- Help them find a role in serving in the ministries of the congregation.

- Introduce them to a small group that will love them and nurture them in their faith journeys.

Celebrate successes with the family. Whenever they reach milestones in the contract, send a note of congratulations and give them a small gift. When the contract is completed, throw a party for the family and the church members close to them to celebrate. Present them with a gift that will serve as a visual reminder of the results of their hard work.

Working with Financially Needy Families in the Community

Churches begin working with financially needy families in the community as a result of referrals. These are occasionally self-referred (someone knocks at the church door), but more typically they come via members or community agencies with whom the church has developed a relationship.

Referral sources will quickly dry up if deacons do not respond in timely ways to the referrals, if the church does not deliver what it says it will, or if deacons or church staff do not maintain a relationship with the referring persons. Deacons need to spend time creating and keeping a flow of needy people coming to the church if the diaconate is to be a ministry-developing office in the church. The churches that have the greatest flow or referrals are those that keep their relationships alive with referral sources, respond quickly to the immediate needs, and regularly report progress for each family referred to both the congregation and the referral sources.

Pam was a single parent. She married immediately after high school graduation.

Within a year Stacy was born, and five months later Pam's husband left her, taking the car and the credit cards. By the time Pam realized what was happening, her husband had left her with car payments and credit debt totaling $17,000. Pam ended up working part-time in a fast-food restaurant and living in government-subsidized housing. She had no purchasing power because of the bad credit rating she inherited. Pam was referred to the church for supplemental food aid and paper products, which she could not purchase with food stamps.

How can deacons best respond to referrals from community agencies?

Following these four principles for aid distribution will help recipients move towards self-sufficiency rather than dependence:

1. God gave people energy and skills to solve their own problems and attain their own dreams. One of the greatest needs among poor people is self-respect stemming from personal accomplishments and successes. Poor people apply their own energies and skills to accomplish their own dreams.

2. Aid will produce better and more lasting results when, instead of temporarily bailing them out, it helps poor people solve their own problems. The most effective aid is friendship, personal encouragement, or information that points poor people to new alternatives and opportunities.

3. Aid will be effective only when it follows comprehensive problem solving. The problems of poor people fall into four categories:

   - Poor people suffer from social isolation and abandonment. They are often separated from those who demonstrate Christian love and acceptance and can help them love themselves.

- Poor people lack a helping infrastructure. They lack connections with people who can help them appropriately analyze and pursue opportunities for self-advancement.

- Poor people often lack adequate employment skills, budgeting skills, childcare skills, and communication skills.

- Poor people often lack necessary resources and funds such as permanent, affordable housing, reliable transportation, telephone service, and newspapers.

When problems in any one of these categories are dealt with in abstraction from the others, poor people seem only to shuffle from one problem to another. The most effective efforts address all of these problems with a single plan.

4. Aid is most effective when it is directed at opportunities rather than at problems. The inclination of most deacons is to prove their benevolence to poor people. This inclination leads them to channel their aid toward the presented problems rather than opportunities that will help the recipients solve their own problems and attain their personal dreams in life. Effective aid points poor people to those activities, changes, skills, and resources that will help them identify and take new steps toward goals in life.

Here is a generic process to follow to help poor people:

1. Pray that God will

   - plant all his loving concern in your heart.

   - direct you to find a volunteer lay minister for this new referral.

   - give you eyes to see and ears to hear the whole story surrounding this referral.

   - use your church to be his healing balm in this referral's life and to bring this person to a saving faith in Christ.

2. Make an initial visit to address the present need. Try to establish a follow-up visit—a time when you can get acquainted and learn more about each other. When giving aid for the first or second time, remember that

   - initial aid is only a door into a relationship.

   - the purpose of giving initial aid is only to remove a person far enough from crisis that he or she can begin to begin solving his or her underlying problems. Poor people will have a tough time addressing goals and opportunities if their basic human needs for food, clothing, housing, health, and security are not met first.

   - limiting the number of aid applications to one or two gifts is best. Further aid will begin a pattern of dependency unless it flows from a mutually-arranged helping plan.

3. Arrange for some acts of kindness from other church volunteers. These are best limited to kind words, visits, cards, invi-

tations for meals, and in-kind gifts (clothes, food, paper products, a bicycle for a child, etc.).

4. Recruit a person or small group of people to minister to this new friend. The recruits are expected to

- pray daily for this family and love them unconditionally.

- meet with them at least weekly (more often at first).

- encourage them to follow their plan.

- stick with them as friends until the Lord closes the door on the relationship (one of them moves away or the recipient shuts them out).

- celebrate victories with them.

5. By the second aid visit,

- introduce the church lay minister.

- begin listening to their life's journey and sharing yours.

- tell the recipient that you care about them, and that you and your church would like to help them set and follow a plan to get off all public assistance and on their own two feet. Ask if they would like that kind of help. If they would, set a time to plan together.

6. Follow the planning steps with the recipient as outlined in Appendix L.

7. Find a place where the recipient's talents can be used in the church. Involvement on their part will help them feel reciprocity for the aid they receive, meet more members, and feel welcome.

8. Turn the plan over to the lay ministers and stay in touch, encouraging them

and supporting them in their new ministry. The ministry is now theirs.

9. Inform the deacons and congregation about progress with the family, always maintaining discretion and confidentiality. Help the church celebrate God at work through his body.

10. Participate in celebrating accomplishments the family makes in its journey.

A policy that limits the number of times a person can receive aid from the church without a ministry plan (usually two or three) is often helpful. Some families will not be interested in working out plans. Providing aid apart from a plan over a long period of time is usually not good stewardship; it typically creates or compounds dependency in recipients and gives a distorted view of what the church is and does. The church is on a mission with limited budgets. It is not another social service agency. Deacons will have to set those boundaries.

Some recipients will not follow their plans. This usually happens when a recipient is not committed to his or her stated goals, or when the goals are unrealistic. Deacons then can renegotiate the plans based on revised goals and dreams, or they can decide to terminate use of benevolent aid. Even if this occurs, a lasting relationship between the mentor and the recipient may eventually draw the family to Christ and his church. One advantage is that deacons don't have to judge recipients' motives. The plan is the objective tool around which to make decisions. If a person doesn't complete the plan, either the plan was wrong or the person no longer needs or wants the aid. The answer to that question always lies with the recipient. Recipients have to face the choices about their own future.

Evangelism in this scenario begins with the prayers of the deacon and the mentor. Opportunities to share Christ are woven into the plan through the natural relationship with the mentor. Opportunities to serve and participate in the church enhance the relationship, and small group ministry strengthens it. Also helpful is a contemporary worship venue, where the recipient does not have to make a culture leap to understand what is happening.

People who experience God's love are often ready to hear about it and often respond in faith to him.

Seven: **Celebrating Results**

An important part of any effort or program—whether new or old—is tracking results and celebrating them. Today's society focuses on performance. Celebrations mark passage from the past to the future. They confirm best efforts and results from past accomplishments, and they point to a still developing but planned future. On both an individual and corporate level, celebrating results is crucial.

Celebration for Confirming and Building Faith

Monica was a single parent with four children. Her husband left her without explanation and without financial support. She had not been employed outside the home for several years and had no viable marketable skills that would earn a sustainable wage for her family. Deacons from a nearby church discovered she was living in her house without water, heat, or electricity and was facing foreclosure on the home. They sat down with her and forged a plan. They would help Monica go to school to become certified as a legal aide; she would work part-time and go to school full-time. Meanwhile, they helped her sell the house, and by working with a local Habitat for Humanity chapter, they were able to build her a new home at an affordable rate of payment.

The deacons helped Monica celebrate when she found a good part-time job. They celebrated again, with a big party, at a ground-breaking ceremony. They invited the media and got great community exposure; community leaders, churches, and a host of business people attended. They threw another party to applaud the milestone of her completion of her first year of school. The deacons also planned celebrations when the house was completed and when Monica graduated.

The significance of this story is that Monica experienced these celebration events as faith-building occasions. People who set goals and achieve them are able to look back and recognize that only God could have designed these paths for them. Monica was headed straight for a life of despair; then God's people entered her life. The celebration events remind everybody that God is in control. These milestones confirmed to Monica that he reigns and loves her personally. Celebrations build faith and draw those who participate closer to him. At several points in these celebrations, both Monica and others testified to God's grace.

Celebrations are as important for an organization as for the individual. Organizations' mission and vision statements, well-crafted plans, and competent staff are good and necessary things; but celebration events give Christian organizations and churches the opportunity to set the record straight. God reigns. His love compels the organization and its members to perform these loving deeds. At his discretion he gives his people strength, power, and resources. He controls the events and resources needed to reach each goal. The self-sacrificing people who volunteer in churches and non-profit agencies often risk burnout. These celebration activities draw them back repeatedly to their reason for being. They renew their faith commitment to God.

Celebration for Recognition

Raising four children alone while working and going to school full-time takes incredible courage. Monica dreamed of self-reliance and becoming a paralegal.

Monica was a fighter and a role model; her determination and hard work called everyone in the community to dream and work hard. Through public celebration activities, the community recognized Monica's accomplishments and made it grow stronger.

The diaconate also grows stronger through these recognition events; they become a symbol of what is good and strong in the community. They earn credibility as an organization that makes a difference, offers hope and help to hurting people, and effectively and competently solves problems. They earn a reputation as a pillar of community cohesion.

Celebration for Motivation

Monica struggled with enormous pressures during this time of transition. Many nights she fell into bed exhausted and wondered if she could keep going. Celebrating each tangible accomplishment strengthened and motivated her to face the next steps of her self-sufficiency plan. She drew pride from her accomplishments and recognized her own courage and stamina.

The same situation applies to deacons. The deacons were overwhelmed when they first began meeting with Monica, but together, step by step, they forged this plan.

The deacons found their congregation and community far more generous than they believed possible. At their first congregational meeting to determine if they could raise funds for building a house, over $20,000 was committed, far surpassing their hopes. Many construction and business owners donated generous amounts of labor and material. In the end, they constructed a home valued at over $80,000 for less than $45,000.

Each celebration point increased the deacons' belief that they could do more. They recognized that Monica was serious about helping herself, so they felt good about helping her. They gained the drive and motivation to keep going. The celebrations built faith in their ability to take a next step and unleashed their willingness to take incrementally larger risks for completing their part of the plan. The deacons were repeatedly surprised at how many people supported them. Celebrations revealed how big their ministry team was; they had a power for ministry they had not recognized before. Celebrations motivate and refresh organizations.

Celebration for Assimilation

Who came to Monica's celebrations? Her deacons came. Her new spiritual parents and their family came. Members of her new church came. People from the community came—especially those who were involved in the building process. Her new neighbors came. Classmates from her college came. These celebration events proved to Monica how many people supported her and how much the community rallied around her. She gained a sense of security and belonging. These celebrations truly built community.

These events also showed the deacons how big their community was. The deacons discovered people they never knew had gifts and interest in ministry. They experienced firsthand the community's tremendous "hands and feet" for ministry.

The deacons discovered that they needed help beyond their own congregation to complete this housing project. Their classis deacons conference gave them access to a whole range of additional tradespeople and construction people. They suddenly became one campus of a larger Christian Reformed congregation. Their "family" of churches offered gifts of all kinds. This served to strengthen the capacity of the diaconal conference overall. Other churches also began to understand that they were not limited to the strength, vision, or resources of their own congregations. They belonged to a broader community of churches.

Another inspiration resulted for the deacons and the congregation. Their church previously had a reputation of taking care of their own but excluding outsiders. This event transformed the congregation's image in the community. Now neighborhood residents developed a new respect for them as a caring church. This was the first step to a number of invitations for involvement in community activities and events.

Celebrations help the person served and the serving organization to assimilate themselves in their communities.

Celebration for Support

Monica was struggling to survive alone before the deacons discovered her plight. Overwhelmed and immobilized, she had no resources or strength to resolve her problems. Recruiting a couple of people to befriend, encourage, and emotionally support Monica proved to be one of the deacons' most fruitful actions. With regular support and encouragement, Monica found the courage and discipline to face each day one at a time. Every point of celebration strengthened these relationships and confirmed Monica's self-worth and resilience.

The celebrations helped her recognize her accomplishments and the value of her hard work. They helped her stay focused on her dreams for a better future for herself and her children. The people who cared deeply about her visited her regularly and often worked beside her. They were Jesus' special representatives to Monica. To her they seemed like Jesus in the flesh.

The deacons, too, had limited resources and vision. They had never taken on a housing project before. They had never even worked long-term with a nonmember before. These times of celebration confirmed them and served as tangible markers of new accomplishments and victories. These points of celebration also increased volunteerism, financial support, and organizational recognition.

At the ground-breaking ceremony, two television stations taped the ceremony and three local papers covered the story. All emphasized the need for additional volunteers and gave updated financial information; most of them interviewed the diaconal leaders. The results included voluntary contributions of time, talent, funds, and increased receptivity in the community when the deacons had to solicit additional donations.

The power of volunteer networks also kicks in after these times of celebration. John was a finish carpenter and cabinetmaker. He had become Monica's friend when he worked on her house. He attended her party to celebrate the end of her first year of college. At the party, someone mentioned the need for some flooring and landscaping. John works with people in those businesses every day, so he recruited volunteer donations and labor for those jobs within the week from his contacts. These celebrations broadened the support network and circle of friends and the number of volunteers grew.

Every celebration event becomes another opportunity to share needs and wishes. They can be strategic venues for increasing support for a person or an organization.

Celebration for Community Building

Probably the most important reason for creating celebration events is to build community. Monica's life was filled with activity. Had volunteers not taken the time to help her pull back on special occasions by organizing and hosting celebration events, she would not have celebrated them. She would not have paused to enjoy her accomplishments and the people who meant so much her. She would not have had the energy to do it. These special events were times of laughter and fun for Monica. She and her friends played games, talked, sang, ate, and celebrated. For a little while, she was able to forget the pressures of life and to relax and enjoy the people who had become her new community.

The deacons and the volunteers reaped the same benefits. They too were busy people and needed these occasions to "fill up" on each other's friendship. They too needed the opportunity to enjoy Monica and one another. They wanted to be community; celebrating together helped them define one another beyond their roles as carpenters, plumbers, deacons, contractors, landscapers, students, and employers. They loved each other, and they needed to enjoy one another as friends.

Celebrations are vital to building community. They help the community grow together in love. They mark passage from a difficult past to a future that is bright because participants join in a loving fellowship. We were created to serve one another and to receive from one another; these celebration events become one of the building blocks for creating and sustaining community.

Eight: **Welcoming and Enfolding**

Our History

A Chapel Legacy

The Christian Reformed Church (CRC) has struggled greatly with evangelism growth. New church planting has added most new members to the denomination. Bringing ethnic congregations into the denomination has also added many new members. By contrast, established churches have shown very little growth (less than 2 percent), and far too many of them have suffered substantial losses in membership. The focus of this chapter is to offer a different approach to established churches— an approach that stimulates growth through intentionally welcoming and enfolding into our congregations people whom we have helped through a range of diaconal ministries.

The Christian Reformed Church enjoys a long and often envied history of missionary support. God has used the CRC to help Reformed denominations in other countries grow larger than itself. Unfortunately, the Christian Reformed Church has taken the same approach to growing the church in North America that it has taken overseas, but with very poor results. For decades the dominant means in the United States and Canada for reproducing the church and bringing others to Christ has been the formation of chapels and new church plants. This legacy was built on the assumption that chapels and new churches could be free to meet unchurched people on their terms. The pastors of these churches were considered missionaries. The denomination granted these churches freedom in organization, worship methods, numbers of services per Sunday, and gender issues that they would not deem suitable in more established churches. The denomination as a whole was a closed system, unwilling to be influenced by people from different backgrounds, traditions, and cultures.

Unchurched people and new converts had relatively little opportunity to influence traditional churches. Missionary churches did not even have "full membership" in classes; they reported to classis through sponsoring congregations. Some of these new churches remained chapels for more than fifty years. A comfortable but unhealthy "us and them" dynamic flourished and perpetuated the denomination's traditional power centers and worship culture. The Christian Reformed culture offered members few engagements with the unchurched world and insulated churches from the influence of these chapels and their leaders. The Christian Reformed Church practiced missions at home the same way it did abroad: through missionary support. The church would pay for them but did not want to truly engage them or be influenced by them.

A Closed Community

While their desire was to stay firm and pure, the Christian Reformed churches were less than faithful to God and his call to be light, salt, and leaven in their own communities.

They were often isolated, separatist, and exclusive communities. Almost every church in the denomination ran identical programs such as Men's Societies, Ladies Guild, Cadets, GEM Girls, Coffee Break, and Men's Life. If churches in Sioux Center, Iowa; Grand Rapids, Michigan; the heart of New York; and Edmonton, Alberta, maintain identical worship culture, organizational structures, and church programs, then a closed culture exists.

The small number of congregations that responds to its community's needs with specially designed ministries also signifies closed church culture. How many Christian Reformed churches host an AA group, a single-parent ministry, or a respite-care program? Only in the last five years have Christian Reformed churches begun paying attention to target and side-door ministries. The new churches and a few of the large churches are leading the way.

An additional sign of a closed community is the small number of church leaders who are relatively new to the church. Closed communities or cultural groups often shield themselves from outside influences. Many Christian Reformed churches require council approval of leaders for all church committees. Criteria for selection of leaders has less to do with identifying people with appropriate gifts for the work than how long someone has been a member and how well they are known. Rarely does someone hold a leadership role if he or she has less than ten years of membership in that congregation.

Amish or Hutterite communities are another example of a closed community or system. They are reluctant to adapt to changes in their environment. For example, some members of these communities still farm completely organically and only with horses. Their worship today closely resembles the worship of fifty or one hundred years ago. Their communal systems work by the same structures and rules as decades ago.

In a similar manner the Christian Reformed Church has been reluctant to add new systems of congregational leadership, new worship patterns, new technology, and new social systems. The CRC is as committee-dominated today as it was fifty years ago. Many congregations select leaders the same way they did forty years ago. Many church offices still do not have computers. Although the CRC's members are at the forefront of change in their business and personal lives, they glean a sense of security in a rapidly changing environment by guarding things in the church from change. To unchurched people, this lack of change has made the church appear out-of-date and incapable of addressing today's problems and issues.

Still another symptom of a closed community and culture is the church working independently of other existing resources for meeting her members' needs. An inner-city church in Grand Rapids, Michigan, found itself reeling under the weight of its ministries to needy inner-city families. They were conducting weekly fresh produce donations to a host of families, helping several families with tuition assistance, responding to literally hundreds of families each year that knocked at their door for various emergency needs, and involving themselves in landlord and tenant disputes. But the greatest drain on them emotionally came from several families who were asking for various types of aid month after month, and in some cases for years. The church rarely consulted caseworkers, mental health workers, social service agencies, or counseling agencies, all of which were eager to help them minister more effectively and efficiently. Many churches in the denomination have never worked with their local community social service organizations.

A Bifurcated Ministry Design and Theory

A recent study (by survey) of deacons conducted by a Calvin seminarian concluded that very few of the unchurched people whom deacons and church members helped ever became members of the church. Deacons even reported a preference to assimilate needy people into churches other than their own to meet their spiritual needs. Their logic goes something like this: "They won't understand our worship or culture; we can't relate to their poverty. They will never be like us. So let's bring them to a church that will understand and accept them. That way they will still become Christians and part of God's church." The church has not wanted to be stained by people from "outside" the prevailing culture. Keeping things the same is more important in the Christian Reformed Church than bringing people to Christ and Christian Reformed congregations.

The same study revealed that many deacons are not convinced that the office of deacon bears any responsibility for evangelism and assimilation. Deacons do not typically receive training in these matters. Evangelism is often considered the work of elders.

A couple of years ago a diaconate from Classis Holland requested consultation. The deacons were discouraged. A young lady in the church repeatedly asked them for funds for housing, transportation, health care, and other daily needs. But all the help (several thousand dollars over a few years) they had given had produced no change in her life. They felt like poor stewards. They told the woman and her live-in companion that their pattern of assistance had to change. Either the aid would help them achieve new skills, employment, or education so that they could be self-sustaining in the future, or it would be discontinued. The woman chose underemployment and dependence, ignoring the many alternatives open to her. At the next council meeting the elders (one of whom was the woman's father) said, "Your job as deacons is to meet her physical needs. We as elders will address her spiritual needs." The deacons rightly believed, however, that their aid was being used as bait to convince the woman and her companion to come to church. This rationale showed little regard for the true welfare of the woman, her future as a dignified person, and her responsibility to live as a full and active kingdom citizen. This was not Christian charity; Christian charity brings healing, wholeness, and healthy interdependence. Separating a message of Christ's love and forgiveness from his design for healthy living makes no sense.

The denomination has practiced a dualistic mission enterprise for years. Even the denominational agencies have separated word and deed ministries via their particular charters and lack of coordination. Why is the relief and development arm of the church not integrated into the mission agencies of the church both locally and abroad? Do congregations need evangelism committees and diaconates? Not if word and deed ministries are integrated. Deacons are rarely asked in the council room or by church visitors if the needy people they help are being assimilated into the congregation.

Holistic ministry by definition means that a person needs help in all spheres of life (physical, spiritual, emotional, social).

People will not experience the fullness of life that God intended for them unless all aspects of their lives are nurtured and balanced. Evangelism and assimilation rarely occur in the absence of a long-term friendship between a caring Christian and an unchurched person. *Appropriate* ministry with people (poor and wealthy) is impossible without getting close to them, committing to be their friends through good times and bad, and helping them grow in all areas of their lives. People most often find balance and healing in the context of a loving and nurturing community of believers. In the context of intimate and honest relationships, people receive encouragement and feedback to adjust to necessary changes.

Unfortunately, deacons have too often brought the gifts of their congregations to people in need through agencies or drop-off visits and neglected to invite recipients into relationships with their Christian community. Deacons have assumed that the greatest need is financial or material. It rarely is. The greatest need is more often a capacity to dream, set goals, experience intimate fellowship and support, and receive honest feedback that enables people to correlate their behavior with the resulting predicaments or successes.

This pattern of helping by giving from a distance also secludes the givers from the blessings they might receive from those helped. Poor people often gain faith, stamina, and emotional strength through adversity. They know more about contentment, sacrificial giving, and sharing than many church members do. They can help members identify their cultural prejudices and illusions. People in need will give to church members as much or more than they take from them if open, close, loving relationships develop.

A Pattern for Evangelism and Assimilation

A recent survey of West Michigan Christian Reformed churches that grew the most through evangelism revealed the following common strategies for evangelizing and assimilating people into the churches:

1. *Connect each member to one person who needs him or her.* Most Christian Reformed members cannot name even one unchurched person with whom they have a close, sustained relationship. Yet clustered around every church in the nation are hundreds of people on welfare rolls, hundreds of isolated elderly people, hundreds of lonely and overwhelmed single parents, hundreds of poor people, hundreds of those who lack education and work skills, and hundreds who cannot read. It could be a fair expectation for every professing member of a Christian Reformed church to befriend one of these people. Every member can be a friend.

Christian Reformed churches will grow if and when members love their neighbors enough to integrate them into their lives and congregations. That will require a shift in the culture and in the criteria for membership in God's church. Currently, membership expectations include assent to doctrinal, creedal, and theological standards, commitment to regular participation in worship, and commitment to live a biblically faithful moral life. What might happen if the church expected that every believer befriend one person who needs him/her and share his/her life, belongings, and faith with them; pray for them daily; and invite them to worship? What would happen if every member were asked yearly whom God has placed in their lives to reach? The church leaders could then make it a principal function of their work to help all members connect to one person who needs them.

Long-term relationships that are characterized by love, care, and support and are open to faith discussion are the bedrock of evangelism and assimilation. Evangelism and assimilation will not occur if members do not commit to becoming God's physical presence—his hands and feet extending love to unchurched people one at a time for as long as the relationship can last.

When I met Robert, he was living in government-subsidized housing with his five-year-old daughter. In my first meeting with Robert, I asked him what he wanted most in life and for his future. His greatest personal need was for safe and affordable housing. His second greatest felt need was an opportunity to grow through education so he could earn a livable wage. His third greatest need was to be part of a caring community where he could feel loved instead of put down. Dean, a member of our congregation, agreed to pray for Robert daily, to talk with him daily (by phone), and to meet with him weekly. He also agreed to partner with him in developing and following a plan that would help Robert achieve his goals and dreams. Four years later, Robert is a member of Dean's congregation. He was loved into it through a holistic ministry design. Dean was the key to it all. He was Christ to Robert, and he pointed the way to life with him.

2. *Add target and side-door ministries.* Social and emotional problems are common to church members and community unchurched people alike. These difficul-

ties include alcoholism, drug addiction, disasters, unwanted pregnancies, spouse abuse, disabilities of family members, loss of family members, daycare needs, housing needs, medical crises, care for elderly, and lack of opportunities for elderly people to serve. Churches are beginning to realize that members' needs can be met through specialty groups formed around common needs. Some of these groups have a Bible study or evangelism component to them (these are target ministries); others do not (these are side-door activities that create a flow of people into the church). Many of these groups are entry points that give churches an opportunity to begin ministering through a need experienced by both members and unchurched people.

Several types of activities characterize target and side-door ministries that assimilate people effectively:

- A strong friendship between a church member and an unchurched person forms during group activities.

- A Bible study or faith-developing component is included.

- Churches use the ministry meetings to deliberately disseminate information to unchurched people who attend. Rita was a member of an AA group that met at a church in Jenison, Michigan. At a weekly meeting, Rita found information on her chair about an upcoming church picnic, next Sunday's worship, and a newly-formed divorce-recovery group. She began attending the divorce-recovery group, which eventually brought her to close relationships with other church members, which in turn led her to attend worship and new members classes. Rita is now an active member in the church.

- When participants complete a cycle of activity with these groups, they are often ready for a specific invitation to join an existing or new small group for fellowship and faith development.

Intentional follow-up with participants in side-door and target ministries often leads to assimilation if one or more of these activities occur.

James was an alcoholic, as was his wife, Sue. They began attending an AA meeting at a Christian Reformed church. At their second meeting they met Ron and Sally, members of the church hosting the AA meetings. All four loved to bowl. Ron and Sally invited James and Sue to join their church bowling league. Seven months later James and Sue became members of a church they hadn't even known existed until they looked for a local AA group. Ron and Sally were the relational key that turned this side-door ministry into a loving community of faith.

3. *Encourage members to invite their friends.* Polls of people who have recently joined a church consistently show that the most frequent reason unchurched people give for attending a church is a friend's invitation to accompany them to a church activity or service. The invitation might be to participate in a church musical or a single-parent group, to meet new neighbors at a youth hockey event sponsored at the church, or to join a sportsman's club run by church members. The event by itself rarely changes people, but the event becomes the gateway for loving Christian relationships and authentic spiritual healing for a person in a time of need.

4. *Involve seekers and new attendees in small groups.* Personal isolation characterizes today's society. People move and switch careers frequently. Professionalism in the workplace often requires relational distance. Extended families live far apart, and people don't know others in their communities well. Service institutions from banks to schools specialize in narrow aspects of people's affairs without getting to know them. People are lonely and isolated.

Churches that create small groups for member care, accountability, and fellowship are ideal places to assimilate newcomers. Church consultants have documented that when a new member is personally connected in a caring relationship with six other adults, he or she is likely to stay. Small groups that offer intimate relationships, unconditional care, material and social support, a safe place to seek direction, and spiritual nurture will meet the needs of members and unchurched people today.

5. *Conduct a six- to twelve-week new members class.* Three advantages stand out for churches who intentionally invite new attendees to join a new members class. First, a new members class creates an arena where new attendees can become intimately familiar with other members. Often the bonds of friendship that begin in these classes become lasting relationships. The second is that the class introduces participants to the dynamics and intimacy of small groups. In addition to studying and learning the life and doctrines of the church, participants share their life's story and faith journey. They feel as though they belong. Many churches today are beginning to add small groups for discipleship, nurturing, and accountability for members. These new member classes model small group life at its best. Encouraging participants to

continue in a small group once the class is ended is a small thing. A third advantage: new members are given opportunity to learn the doctrines of the church, to understand its expectations for members, and to discover how the church functions.

Dolly had been burned in her last church, so she stopped attending. She and her husband went through a messy divorce, and people in the church seemed to side with him. She felt cut off and bruised. She even experienced hostility and hatred—at least that's the way she perceived it. Dolly planned on not going to church again for a long time, if ever. But her sister ached to see Dolly experience the kind of church life she had: one that was fulfilling, affirming, and spiritually renewing. She persuaded Dolly to attend church with her, and Dolly found the worship edifying and the community loving. She decided to talk with the pastor, who invited her to attend the new members class where she could get acquainted with the church's doctrine and life with no obligation to join the church. The group welcomed Dolly with such warmth that she joined the church at the conclusion of the class. She also joined several other class members in a new small group for support, accountability, and fellowship.

6. *Provide a contemporary worship venue.* Entering a typical Christian Reformed worship environment is a tremendous cultural leap for someone who has not been to church since childhood, who thinks of the *Readers Digest* as a contemporary Christian magazine, who thinks that Cosby is a Christian television drama, who listens all day to country-western music on the radio, who thinks Moses was a disciple (or never heard of him), and who believes that the

Exodus is an Egyptian. These are characteristics of people who call themselves unchurched Christians; many others have even less exposure to Christ and his church.

Christian Reformed churches have often taken the approach that their way is right and good. If people want to join, they should behave and become like us. This attitude is a less than user-friendly approach to reaching unchurched people. Christian Reformed churches need to help newcomers reach the point where they understand and appreciate their church culture. That will require adding some worship, fellowship, and need-meeting venues that unchurched people can experience without having to make such a great culture leap.

Many people are coming to a faith in Christ and appreciation of the Reformed faith through seeker-sensitive services offered on Saturday evenings or as second Sunday services. These services are characteristically different than traditional services in musical instrumentation and leadership (praise teams rather than choirs) and in choice and style of songs. They also include preaching that uses parables more than exegesis; and drama, poetry, and other contemporary media relating to the theme of the service.

Note: Adding a seeker-sensitive worship service at another time is less difficult than attempting to change the existing worship patterns of a church.

Mary went to church until the age of four when her parents divorced. She grew up knowing nothing about Jesus and the church. She married and had five children. When her youngest was four months old, her husband left her. For almost ten years she scraped by. Then she met Jim. She fell head over heels in love with him, and they married. Jim also had two children from a former marriage. Jim and Mary both worked, and life took on a new pace and routine. They both found themselves talking occasionally about the meaning of life and their purpose in it. Two years later they moved to Jim's childhood community for better career opportunities.

Jim was raised in a Christian home, and somehow God was impressing on him some of the values he had been raised with. Jim and Mary decided to look for a church where they could recommit themselves to God. They attended several churches but were turned off by the formality and the rigidity. Then they attended a Christian Reformed church that had just begun a contemporary service. They found a musical style that they enjoyed, a diversity that mirrored their experiences in life (no Sunday was the same in setup, liturgy, musical leadership, or style), and an informality that matched their lifestyle. Their spirits lifted. The parable style of preaching touched their life experiences and injected into them a new framework for meaning and hope. After a few months of visiting, they both said, "We love this church; we need it." They went through a membership class and joined the church. Within two months, Jim, an avid archer, was talking about starting a new sportsmen's club to help draw others to the church. Mary was already befriending two lonely young women who had been fringe members for a long time.

God's Spirit alone can change people. But church members today have untold opportunities to care enough about a needy neighbor to embody Christ for them—to be his hands and feet. Jesus promises to hear their prayers and give them far more than they imagined if they submit to him.

God requires sacrificial living. To some extent, Christians have to allow the mission of the church to shape them and their congregational lives rather than expect unchurched people to conform to their image and practices. That was the heart of God's condemnation of the Pharisees in Jesus' day. The Christian Reformed Church today has to adapt its mission frontier and methods if it cares about bringing unchurched people to Christ and holistic healing.

Nine: **The Changing Environment**

For every McDonalds, the United States has fifty-three churches (three hundred thousand Protestant and twenty thousand Catholic). There are enough churches to reach every American for Jesus. The problem is that not enough churches have vision, strategies, and plans to reach the unchurched. Congregations are so busy ministering to themselves and competing with one another for members that they ignore opportunities to reach unchurched people. They tightly guard the boundaries of their religious cultures and worship practices. They have lost their ability to see and respond appropriately to people who need Jesus.

The Culture Context

American culture is changing rapidly. Here are some significant changes occurring right now. *Note: this information is adapted from a workshop entitled* Understanding Ministry in a Changing Culture *by George Barna.*

The population is growing, but not just from childbirth. Childbirth rates continue to slowly and steadily decline about 1 percent every ten years (currently 9 percent of population growth). Up to one million immigrants (half are illegal aliens) enter this country annually. A high percentage of them are young and are in or close to childbearing ages. In many metropolitan areas minorities are now majority cultures. Population growth projections for the U.S. are for Caucasian growth to be 5 percent,

African American 15 percent, Asian American 45 percent, and Hispanic American 39 percent.

People are highly transient and mobile today. Fifteen to twenty percent of the population will move annually. Metropolitan areas are growing fastest, even beyond the current 78 percent of people living in metro areas.

Americans are graying. Life expectancy is currently seventy-eight years and may be close to ninety in another ten years. Of all North Americans who have ever lived beyond sixty-five, over half are living today. They are causing many transitions:

- Retirement ages are rising.

- Changes in employment relationships are occurring: sabbaticals, retraining, phased retirements, part-time hours.

- Environmental adaptations are increasingly necessary: typefaces must be larger, traffic lights more visible, diets and menus adjusted, flooring changed (carpets instead of hard surfaces).

- Heightened generational conflicts are inevitable.

- Wealth transfer: by 2020 there will be a massive transfer of accumulated wealth from older people. Much of it will not go to children.

- Elder care: both third-party care and multigenerational households will grow substantially.

Education is valuable but of dubious quality. Functional illiteracy is staggering. Forty-nine percent of the population in the United States and about 40 percent of the population in Canada cannot function above a seventh- or eighth-grade level. The United States is now forty-ninth in adult literacy among 158 U.N. countries. High school dropout rates are staggering. Close to a million graduates last year could not read at a seventh-grade level.

Educational quality continues its decline. Among industrialized nations, the teacher/pupil ratio is the fourth worst in the United States, and test scores continue to decline. College education is expected to rise in cost to $100,000 for a four-year degree by the year 2000. Meanwhile, corporations are taking over the education of their workforces. While more students are going to college, the proportion of people with degrees will decrease. Women now account for half of all degrees earned.

The national economy is being reinvented. The banking industry is currently being reinvented. We have moved from the industrial/production age to a service-based information age. There will be a projected thirty-four times more raw information available by 2005 than in 1990. Small business is the present and the future. Bankruptcy is now considered a strategic response to financial crises rather than a failure. Women are major players in business. Women start five out of six new small businesses. Careers are fluid. Those citizens born between 1965 and 1983 are likely to change careers six to twelve times in their lifetimes. Poverty is widespread and growing. Most poor people live in the cities where costs are highest. By government standards, there are thirty-five to forty million poor people today. The working poor is the fastest growing segment of the poor population. Crime is epidemic. Six out of ten adults change their lives out of fear. Ninety-nine percent of adults will be victims of crime. Ten percent of the criminals produce 90 percent of crimes. Communities across the country are struggling with the costs of incarceration.

The family is being redefined. The standard definition of family is now "all who deeply care about me." Single-parent homes have increased by 40 percent since the 1960s. Almost one-fourth of all young adults are now living with their parents. More of the elderly are being cared for by their children. Cohabitation is rising even though most people believe in marriage. The majority of those in first-time marriages will have lived together, even though studies have shown that cohabitation increases the chance of divorce by 82 percent. Those citizens born between 1965 and 1983 have a 200 percent increase in the incidence of cohabitation. Abuse is on the rise, fifty times more likely among those who cohabit.

Most people believe in marriage, but one in three believes sex with consenting adults is all right and that marriage should not limit partners' choices. Fifty percent claim that divorce is acceptable if the marriage is not working. Little commitment is left in marriage. Twenty-six percent of all adults who have been married have divorced (Christians have similar rates). Married women with children who divorce retain their expenses, but their income typically drops 50 percent. Births out of wedlock continue to rise. In 1994, 33 percent of children were born to single mothers.

Homosexuality is overstated. Approximately 1 percent of the population practices homosexuality.

Childhood is different today. Over $20 billion is spent on childcare annually. First-time parents are substantially older than a decade ago. Kids today are influenced more by friends, peers, and the media than by their parents.

- Twice as many kids since 1970 are not living with both of their natural parents.

- Almost 400,000 babies are born to unwed women nineteen years of age or younger annually.

- Forty percent of all pregnancies among women fifteen to nineteen end in abortion.

- Suicide rates among ten- to fourteen-year-olds have risen 88 percent in the past decade.

- Substance abuse is common, especially alcohol consumption.

- More than three million children are abused each year.

- Over 600,000 juveniles are held in custody.

- Fifteen million juveniles live in poverty.

- Gangs are replacing families as the center of care for children.

The list goes on. Consider the changes coming to welfare, crime, politics, and medical care. Almost all major social institutions and programs of the last twenty years are changing significantly.

The Organization Context

America's organizational life today is being reshaped along with all other dimensions of people's lives. **Bigger is better.** Consider the following:

- While small business is the new cornerstone of the economy, big institutions retain control of incredible assets. Americans are comfortable receiving services from big institutions as long as the quality is excellent. Recent mergers have led to megabusinesses in health care, finance, entertainment, and telecommunications. Many basic services today are dispensed and controlled under the umbrella of large organizations. At the same time, trust in large institutions has eroded to unprecedented levels. Loyalty to big name products or companies has disappeared. Every company today has to continually earn the support of its markets.

- Schools across the country are significantly larger as the result of the concentration of American suburbs. Even rural schools are no longer village schools, but have been replaced with consolidated district schools.

- The size of the American farm has doubled from 195 acres in 1945 to 465 acres in 1992.

- Retail stores are now large stores. Many are affiliated with large chain stores.

- The size of university enrollments has steadily increased.

- The size of the government mirrors the incredible growth of the federal budget (and deficit).

The distinct advantages of being big include ready access to resources, unprecedented network capacity, technical competence, cost efficiencies, and an incredible spectrum of input and output choices.

Small is necessary too. Consider the following:

- Information today is accessible but so voluminous and complex that the next generation of institutional opportunities will come through smaller technical niches in the institutional arena. Even within large companies, employees will have to operate in small diversified units in order to satisfy the technical demands of the company and to earn repeatedly the respect and trust of the marketplace.

- The population distrusts government today. It is too big, impersonal, and removed from the people's daily experiences. So while society today is willing to grant to government the management of a few basic services, people are clamoring for local control over distribution of funds and program design. The smallest unit of government and the one closest to the local community has the greatest public trust and support.

The big will have to act small to compete with small organizations. Small organizations and businesses have the advantages of familiarity and intimacy, technical competence in niche (narrow) markets, and high trust. In the culture of big things, these will still attract a significant following.

Networking is the new strategy to forge tomorrow's success. Fueled by massive amounts of technical information, new insights and discoveries become possible through cross-functional teams and through networking with technical experts from a variety of sources. Government, business, industry, and service institutions are developing joint venture arrangements and spinning off new, smaller, niche-serving organizations at a phenomenal pace.

The Postmodern Context

Underlying all this change, some significant philosophical shifts are shaping the culture.

1. During the Enlightenment, people had little need for God; they depended on human reason to produce the right answers to society's questions. Today people recognize multiple truths. Human reason no longer leads to a single truth. Seventy-one percent of the population says that two people who have conflicting ideas on a subject can both be right. Truth and moral absolutes do not exist; nothing can be known for certain except that which one experiences.

2. During the Enlightenment, the self-reliant individual was most important. No one really needed anyone else. Today people live in limited community with others, and together they define what is true for them. This tribalism allows truth to be defined differently in differing communities.

3. During the Enlightenment, the processes of scientific discovery (trial and error, cause and effect) gave society the answers it sought. Truth could be found through applying scientific discovery techniques. Today, virtual reality allows people to create their own truths. Fact and fiction blur as people create and recreate their own truths.

4. Human progress marked the Enlightenment. But the legacy that society faces today is tragedy and human misery. Instead of ever-increasing wealth and prosperity, we struggle with war, starvation, AIDS, personal isolation, racism, and incredible human pain. Society today experiences a void of meaning in the midst of all human misery.

The Religious Context

Christianity is not the dominant faith system in America. People slice and dice from various faith systems to find what's "right" for them. Syncretism is the dominant system. The majority of people going to church are not Christians. Many have been inoculated with Jesus but never introduced to him. While seven out of ten people claim to be religious, and two out of three say they believe in God, they do not embrace the Bible as truth. Christianity is not the dominant way for living with God and humankind. Religion in America has become a means for upgrading oneself. People expect religion to provide stability in a context of change and personal difficulty. They also expect religion will give them guidelines for successful living (prosperity) and a place to build relationships that will enhance their influence and prestige. The majority of people today believe the local church is irrelevant to their experience.

The **troops in the church** are illiterate on biblical matters.

- Eighty-two percent believe that "God helps those who help themselves" is in the Bible.

- Seventy-two percent say there is no absolute truth.

- Sixty-three percent cannot name the four gospels.

- Fifty-eight percent cannot name half of the commandments.

- Fifty-eight percent do not know that Jesus preached the Sermon on the Mount.

- Fifty-two percent do not know that the book of Jonah is in the Bible.

Twenty-five percent of the population is **unchurched.** These people have not been to church within six months except for a wedding or funeral. If you add to that the number of people who are nominally churched (go on occasion), the percentage jumps to 50 percent of the population. Why don't people attend church? To them it seems irrelevant, without perceived value. But fewer than one in five are hard-core unbelievers. Eighty percent are open to having the church play some role in their lives. Eighty percent of unchurched people have had some negative experience that drove them out of the church. Most drop out between the ages of eighteen and twenty-five. The unchurched tend to be younger than the norm, more educated, single, and white. They are affluent and sophisticated, and they have a higher incidence of cohabitation outside marriage and loss of family values. They wonder what benefits the church holds for them and are very concerned with the judgmental attitude in the church.

Dreams of the Unchurched

Good health—92 percent

Close personal friendships—74 percent

Purpose for living—72 percent

Comfortable lifestyle—71 percent

Live to old age—55 percent

Live close to family—54 percent

Active sex life—49 percent

Close relationship with God—48 percent

High-paying job—41 percent

Influence to others—29 percent

Fame or recognition—9 percent

Personal Needs of the Unchurched

Financial—32 percent

Career, employment, job issues—
14 percent

Personal health—10 percent

Family issues—7 percent

Unchurched people believe they cannot be forgiven and that God does not hear or answer prayer. They do believe in some god-force, but fewer than 50 percent understand a Christian view of God. Fewer than half believe in a judgment, and two of three do not believe in Satan. They do not distinguish or differentiate between churches. One is not better or worse than another. Most do not care about their own spirituality; it seems irrelevant. A look at their religious activities during a typical month reveals the following:

- Seventy-two percent prayed to God.

- Twenty-seven percent watched a religious TV program—Paul Harvey.

- Twenty-seven percent read the Bible.

- Twenty-four percent read a religious book or magazine—*Reader's Digest.*

- Twenty percent listened to a religious radio program.

- Four percent attended a small group Bible study.

If they were to return to a church, unbelievers would want to experience benefits, knowledgeable believers, tolerance, caring people, concern for the downtrodden, and professionalism/excellence in programs.

The Christian Reformed Church Context

Many Christian Reformed churches are out of touch with their communities. Almost all their programs are designed for believers. Relatively few activities have been designed or modified to reach unchurched Harry and Jane down the street.

The Christian Reformed Church has a historical growth record of less than 1 percent per year through 1994. The denomination would have declined numerically had it not been for internal growth through childbearing. Since 1963 more people have transferred out of the denomination than have transferred in, and our evangelism growth has never measured up to the denomination's goal of 2 percent. 1995 brought an additional loss of almost 20,000 members due to dissatisfaction with issues such as women in office.

Christian Reformed members have developed their own distinct culture. They are reluctant to see it change. Some even equate it with being Christian, to the exclusion of those who do not practice it. The culture can generally be characterized by activities such as traditional worship twice on Sunday, abstaining from business on Sunday, participation of children and adults in Christian schools and their societies (including Christian colleges), and participation at least once midweek in additional instruction at church. Extended family fellowship was once an expectation, and many members still live near and interact weekly with extended family members. Social activities center on family and church friendships and tend to be fellowship and entertainment focused, or exclusive of service and witness.

Other criteria for faithfulness to the culture have been fast disappearing: tithing income, practicing private devotions daily, and conducting family devotions at mealtimes. This culture of religion, while confirming good behavior, contributes to the isolation of Christian Reformed people from unchurched people around them. Many members cannot name one unchurched person with whom they have a close relationship. Many members have never invited an unchurched person to attend their church, while some have invited unchurched people to attend a church other than their own. Christian Reformed members realize unchurched people would have to take a culture leap to feel comfortable among them. For them, retaining comfort in their culture is more important than adjusting or changing it to accommodate people searching for life with Jesus and his body.

What does all of this mean for Christian Reformed churches?

Strategic Planning

Currently, only a small percentage of churches have a regular cycle of strategic planning for their ministries. Of those that do, many have failed in the crucial step of defining a vision—a picture of God's preferred future for their church. Churches tend to do community demographics studies and then ignore the information. Too many churches design new plans to keep the core members comfortable by focusing on their needs or preferences. If they are not vision-driven and strategic in their planning, churches, whether large or small, will lose their members. Congregations have to make hard choices about who they are and what God is calling them to accomplish. The traditional Christian Reformed culture will not reproduce itself fast enough to be self-sustaining.

Entry Points

Although a growing number of new target and side-door ministries are designed to meet members' needs, far too few entry points and programs are available for unchurched people. The front door of many congregations is only open on Sundays and possibly one day midweek. Those options are not very user-friendly for the unchurched people described above. Can Christian Reformed churches plan and design programs to meet community members' needs? The concept is largely untested.

Churches' Polity and Organizational Life

The church needs to adapt itself to the organizational culture of the day.

- If every elder would evangelize one household during each term of service, almost six thousand new households would join the church every three years. Elders are called to evangelize, but too often don't.

- If every deacon would work with one poor family during a three-year term of service and minister in word and deed, drawing the family through deeds of mercy and loving relationship into the body, the church would grow another six thousand families every three years. But most deacons don't.

- A high percentage of congregations have evangelism committees. If half of the churches have an evangelism committee with an average size of four members, and if every member evangelized one family per year, the denomination would grow by at least another two thousand members. But most evangelism committee members don't.

- Social justice committees, deacon auxiliary committees, missions committees, and service committees are all part of the denominational fabric for ministry. Few result in members joining.

Officebearers, including pastors, are supposed to lead by example and should encourage others to do evangelism and diaconal ministry. But the focus of office has been on wielding authority rather than leading service/witness ministry. In several parables, Jesus takes the church leaders to task for their empty rituals and roles. Can we learn from this?

The focus of committees has been on activities rather than on the next person or family God is calling the church to reach. The proliferation of committees is a prime case of expending precious volunteer time and energy on activities that bear no results (a sign of an ineffective organization). Christian Reformed churches need to develop leader-driven, flexible organizational models that focus the church on the mission and vision.

Denominational Support

Denominational agencies—from the mission and ministry agencies to the seminary and publications—have to plan for eroding trust and a declining need for their services. Churches have ready access to almost any kind of service from a host of competing sources. The only reasons for their continued existence are excellence in services, high trust earned through responsiveness to the churches' needs, and distinctive theology. The focus of support for congregations has to shift more to regional agencies.

Church Size

A growing number of large and mega-churches offer a wide array of services. Meanwhile, trust and support for denominational agencies are significantly declining. Many church members are more comfortable in the intimacy of small churches rather than in large ones. Small churches will probably never disappear from the landscape. They will never be full-service churches on a competitive footing with large churches and will not be able to compete with large-church staffing ratios. Large churches, on the other hand, will not be able to retain members without creating small group or cell units for building intimacy, trust, and a sense of belonging. Large churches will experience greater transience in their membership. They will be able to creatively network with a broader spectrum of organizations by virtue of their size, while small congregations will have the edge in niche ministries.

What we've been looking at in this chapter is a gloomy picture of a denomination largely out of touch with a changing world. The Christian Reformed Church has been so preoccupied with perpetuating the dominant culture and with internal issues that it has all too often ignored its place as God's missionary enterprise in the community. Diaconal ministries (ministries of mercy) are a significant piece of the church's work in engaging unchurched people. Diaconal ministries can help churches reengage their communities. The next chapter offers some ideas about how diaconal ministries can help.

Ten: **Emerging Paradigms for Compassion Ministries**

Marti, a crack-addicted, single mother of four children, has a prison record. She has custody of two of her children, both unruly teens. Because of her neglect, the other two children are in foster care. She depends on welfare, although she completed high school and worked for three years as a hospital clerical worker. She knows her life is a mess and wants to change it. What kind of church can effectively minister to Marti?

Aleisha is a fifty-four-year-old mother of six. She lives in a shelter for abused women and children. Her children are grown, and all but one are independent. Her husband of thirty-five years was alcoholic and abusive; she finally moved out when she realized her life was at stake if she did not. Now she is afraid. She is afraid of him and afraid of life. She does not know how to handle bills or money because he never let her learn. He checked the receipt every time she shopped to make sure she did not pocket the change. Before she came to the shelter, she had not been out of the house without him in twelve years. What kind of church can minister effectively to Aleisha, and for that matter to her abusive husband?

Jim was an alcoholic but a skilled worker in a furniture-making business. He sobered up, yet his life progressively worsened. His wife divorced him, and one of his sons was placed in foster care because of his violent behavior. His wife began taking their youngest son to hospitals and doctors with fabricated illnesses. She ran up huge debts

in unnecessary medical bills. Then she sued him for stalking and unbelievable acts of spouse abuse. Jim was in and out of court, paying for all kinds of bills that she incurred. His credit rating plummeted, and the courts did not hold her accountable for her behavior. He was distraught and angry, and he thought repeatedly of killing his mentally-ill wife. What kind of church can minister effectively to Jim?

Sandy and Randy appeared to be a model family in their community. A dental surgeon, Randy earned a big salary. His hobby was hunting wild game. He hunted all over the country and frequently traveled to Africa, Asia, Europe, and Russia for big game. On one such excursion he met and fell in love with a Russian woman. They began an affair. He did not try to hide it from Sandy and his three daughters, but he claimed to love them too. He wanted the best of both worlds. Sandy was reluctant to separate from him. She thought she still loved him. What kind of church can minister effectively to this family?

How can the Christian Reformed Church best help poor and needy people, like those described above, change their lives and bring them to Christ? Here are some things that characterize diaconally active churches today:

1. *Deacons are establishing relationships with organizations in their communities that screen and refer needy people to them for help.* This method has no substitute. These

churches realize many members have no other reasonable way to connect to poor people.

2. *Deacons are learning how to help poor and needy people define their dreams for themselves.* They then develop contracts that outline mutually negotiated steps to reach those dreams. This process usually includes using church mentors for encouragement and friendship, and church resources for incremental incentives to reach the changes.

3. *Deacons are increasing the number of side-door and target ministries to meet members' needs and to draw a flow of non-members to the church.* These ministries are often an entry point to relationships between members and nonmembers, while they also focus on healing for the members. These groups include AA, abuse recovery, support groups for families with mental illness, cancer support groups, and single-parent support groups.

4. *Deacons are inviting recipients of aid to participate in their small groups or even forming small groups around them.* Small groups are ideal for developing friendships, support, and accountability. They naturally assimilate unchurched people.

Several paradigm shifts will significantly strengthen diaconally active churches.

From Elections to Gift-Based Selection

Report 44 (a report on office and ordination) in the 1973 *Acts of Synod* , though not formally adopted by Synod, has given the denomination a basis for changing its idea of leadership in the church. The report acknowledged that offices of the church are God's gifts to the church for equipping members for service. No office is superior or inferior to another. They differ in function only, and they all exist to equip the members for their service to God and his church.

Culture today recognizes specialization in almost every business and workplace. The information explosion has driven this trend toward specialization and applies equally in the church. Some members are gifted to be teachers, some youth leaders, some small group leaders, and others worship leaders. Each role in the church has become specialized with a wealth of resources, information, and training available for the workers. God has gifted every member differently. Members' contributions to church life will have more impact if members serve in their areas of gifts. Their morale will be significantly higher and the burn-out rate significantly lower if the church implements gift-based selection of leaders for all functions in the church. Terms of service can be lengthened, resulting in long-term technical skill retention among workers. Long-term skilled workers can mentor newer workers.

If this principle of gift-based selection is applied to diaconal ministries (and all positions in the church), the church can develop tenured leaders for ministry to abuse victims, multi-problem families, low-income single parents, the grieving, and many others. Two- or three-year terms for members in these technical roles are self-defeating. The technical skill does not develop sufficiently and is not passed on from one deacon to the next.

If churches would help every member analyze his or her gifts for ministry and begin application processes for leadership selection, lay people would flourish in their areas of service with minimal staff support.

From Dualistic to Integrated

Somewhere in its recent history, the Christian Reformed Church has misapplied its polity, driving a wedge between word and deed in ministry. Why are elders nominated first for election? Why are most deacons young family men? Why do people expect deacons to "graduate" into elders? Why do pastors regularly meet with elders and not with deacons? Why are the regional and national diaconal ministries not fully integrated into the life of the broader assemblies?

Deacons and their ministries are marginalized by their absence from the broader assemblies. The mission is bifurcated when home mission committees and diaconal committees do their planning separately. (Can you think of a more significant way for a church to grow than by deacons linking and supporting members in ministries to poor families in the community or by starting a new target ministry?) Deacons do not have access to ministry shares for their ministries, while other mission enterprises do. Why are deacons not represented in the mission activities of the broader assemblies? Doesn't it make sense to add staff to the ministries that link members to unchurched people?

Governance in the church has taken on an unhealthy character because it is divorced from the ministry activities of the assemblies. The office of elder and the broader assemblies have focused on authority to the exclusion of service/witness.

The office of deacon is a high calling. This function is as necessary to the life of the church as any other. Diaconal ministries are pathways to experiential Christianity and bring God's grace to those who need it. Also, middle- and upper-income churches need to learn some valuable lessons from poor people: how to live on less, how to find contentment apart from consumption, how to trust God for their needs, how to share, how to make real sacrifices.

This division of ministry is most poignant when elders tell deacons, "You take care of their physical needs; we, the elders, will care for their spiritual needs." Ministry is not lodged in office; Christ mandates ministry to every believer. The offices exist to equip the saints for service. The theory of separation is abuse of office by such elders on three counts:

- It is dualistic theology, placing more value on people's souls than their bodies and their physical environments.

- It insults deacons who care about the whole person but are told they may not.

- It degrades the person helped because it leads to the perpetuation of dependency. In almost every circumstance of this kind of behavior, such elders limit accountability for behavioral change, or they use aid as bait for conversion.

When a member works with a welfare-dependent single mother, the member does not care only about her physical needs. The member cares about her body, her emotions, her job skills, her spiritual journey, and all aspects of her life. In short, the member loves the woman completely, as a whole person, just as Christ does. The deacon who creates the link between these two, and supports the member in her ministry, is a key leader in the church.

Some deacons today have a vision of every member serving one poor or needy person. That would revolutionize the church as we know it. Working with poor people changes Christians. It shifts their priorities and the weight they place on less significant issues in the church. They consider what it would take to make the church user-friendly to the person they are helping. They are open to letting God's mission shape them. Members would grow in Christ.

Maybe the time has come to rethink office. Perhaps *office* should refer only to Christians who sacrifice deeply for members and ministries. Maybe office should follow function and service already rendered. Past ministry performance could be a criterion for office. At the very least, the church needs a unified ministry leadership system for ministry development rather than the current disjoined system.

From Single-Cell to Multi-Cell

Many church members think of church as the total body of believers who gather together for worship on a Sunday morning. Worship, fellowship, member care, education, and other functions of the church are organized to meet everyone's needs in the largest corporate environment possible. Churches tend to offer one worship environment, one large adult education class, fellowship events that include as many members as possible, and member care systems built on districts. People expect uniformity in programming.

Unfortunately, this method of programming assumes that members are alike, with similar needs and desires, and that everyone should fellowship and worship together. For midsize and large congregations, organizing activities and events around a homogenous principle no longer works; it limits effective ministry and church growth.

Churches that offer more options for more people will flourish beyond those that organize around single cell (homogenous) groups, activities, or events. A church that can offer multiple worship alternatives, care

in small groups, diverse education options, fellowship opportunities, service opportunities, and witness opportunities will meet more people's needs than single-cell churches.

In some churches today, the small group is the place for spiritual growth, accountability, fellowship, care, and service. The small group is the basic unit of organization, and all programming is designed to meet the needs that arise from small group leaders. Corporate worship becomes the celebrative gathering of the congregations.

Diversity is a reality today. People are different and have different needs. They are motivated by different opportunities to serve. Churches that diversify programming at all levels will reach more people than single-cell churches.

From Isolation to Network

Every community in this country has people and institutions with expertise in a full range of social service skills and healing technologies. For the church to duplicate them would not be good stewardship, and to ignore them is also inappropriate. Poor and needy people need the skills and resources of the experts to speed them ahead to a different future.

Church members have one commodity that these institutions cannot offer and most professionals are unwilling to give. The core ingredient missing in today's recovery schemes, the primary agent for sustainable change, is a long-term loving relationship characterized by honesty and care. This kind of relationship says, "No matter what you do to yourself or to others, what condition you are in, or where you are, I will love you and give you honest feedback and encouragement at least once a week for no less than an hour."

In most cases, poor and needy people have been personally abandoned, psychologically defeated, and often abused. They have not learned to love themselves as God loves them. Their self-esteem is low, and their hopes for the future are either undeveloped or presumed impossible. The key to sustainable change is unconditional love and support.

Churches will increase their ministries dramatically when they begin to network with existing organizations because

- the agencies can provide links to poor and needy people that churches cannot produce on their own.

- the churches will use a host of technical resources available only through partnerships.

- through networking, churches can gain a host of additional resources— particularly goods and services—without having to pay for them.

- by serving with organizations in the community, the church will enhance her image as a relevant institution in the community, an institution that cares for people.

Getting Past Relief

Most congregations and deacons who meet a Marti, Aleisha, or Jim do not know how or where to begin a ministry to them. They care about them and are willing to give to them, but they rarely help them make sustainable changes in their lives. Their own need to give is strong; they will give goods and services knowing these will encourage no lasting change. Giving (often foolishly) characterizes churches' responses to needy people.

Giving is most helpful when

- it follows comprehensive diagnosis and screening of recipients.

- a relationship is established first.

- it is used as a catalyst or reward and stimulates behavioral accomplishments—builds on what the recipient first does for himself or herself.

- it is monitored carefully, and feedback is quick and honest.

- it is one piece of a full plan that the recipient has drawn up to attain a different future.

The gift without the giver is usually bare and brutal. The gift by itself creates dependence, distance, and hostility.

Relational ministries such as mentors, small groups, and self-help groups more effectively change behaviors than handouts do. Every church that wants to grow would do well to establish multiple target and side-door ministry groups rather than spend much money on relief and handouts. Churches should ask Marti, Aleisha, Jim, Sandy, and Randy what they want to be different in their lives and then should commit to helping them begin their new journeys.

From Mono-Cultural to Multi-Cultural

The fabric of North American society is increasingly multicultural, incorporating people groups from all over the globe. But we are engaged in the dangerous trends of isolating people groups in ethnic specific communities and building identity around race and ethnicity. When identity is viewed as a gift to all, this can be healthy; the danger comes when it is a unifying force against others.

In a corollary trend, traditional cultural groups huddle together in fear and isolation from the new people groups. Contrary to public sentiment, immigrants and refugees contribute more to the economy and tax base than they draw from it. The assumption that immigrants are anything but an asset to their communities is false.

Churches have been among the most segregated communities and Sundays the most segregated day of the week in our society. Churches that want to be leaders in ministry must embrace and celebrate diversity at every level. Opportunities to do this include voluntarily instituting affirmative action plans and hiring practices, actively seeking and welcoming new members from beyond their ethnic and cultural traditions, continuing to resettle refugees, and standing up for the "stranger" in their community.

From Low-Commitment to High-Commitment Churches

A key difference between growing churches and languishing churches is the level of involvement of members in the ministries of the church. Compare the two.

High-Commitment Churches

1. Help members discover their gifts and then deploy members in areas of their gifts and passions for service.

2. Run programs every day of the week and often run multiple programs simultaneously.

3. Use task forces and short-term leadership groups to create new ministries.

4. Drop some programs every year because they do not have leaders to run them or because they are not successful. Add new ministries every year.

5. Have high levels of giving and chronic budget shortfalls.

6. Have diversified income streams.

7. Have high lay participation in worship.

8. Give generously to a variety of mission causes.

9. Have members that are involved and accountable to one another via small groups.

10. Have high participation in nonformal education opportunities.

Low-Commitment Churches

1. Hope people will get involved and often coerce people to serve.

2. Are locked up except Sunday and maybe one day of the week.

3. Are run by committees.

4. Have the same programs year after year. Offer the programs prescribed by the denomination.

5. Have low levels of giving and usually meet budgets.

6. Have one budget and one dominant income stream.

7. Have low lay participation in worship.

8. Give generously to one or two mission causes.

9. Leave the authority and accountability to the pastors and elders.

10. Have low participation in education events and programs.

The key difference in high accountability churches is an expectation and system that holds members accountable for involvement based on their gifts. The underlying premise is that Christians want to grow and make a difference. The church leadership recognizes their job to help members find out where they can best serve, grow, and contribute to the ministries of the church.

From Diaconal Ministries to Christian Community Development

Christian Community Development Organizations (CCDOs)

CCDOs usually begin when a church pastor, a church school class, or a group of church members commit themselves to being agents of change in their communities. Most begin with people-centered activities, such as youth programs, support groups, food pantries, and clothing distribution activities. Not long into the process, the group often realizes that while these activities are worthwhile, they are not bringing sustainable change to the lives of individuals or to the total health of the community. They begin to study root causes of community disintegration. As churches, they attempt to meet deeper needs in housing, racial reconciliation, crime, and employment. Soon they realize they need greater participation from the community itself and from other churches in the community, and they need resources from inside and outside the community that are not accessible to most churches. That leads to the formation of CCDOs, Christian nonprofit organizations that take responsibility for redeeming broken people and their communities.

The Relationship of a Church to a CCDO

CCDOs lie on a spectrum from tightly integrated to loosely integrated organizations with the churches that produced them. A CCDO that is tightly integrated with a church usually includes in its bylaws a stipulation that many board positions will be filled only with members of the church, and the CCDO leaders are usually recognized as official leaders in the church. Church members retain high control over the programs and policies of the CCDO. In a loosely integrated situation, the church may be asked to regularly represent the faith-based community through symbolic roles (leading prayer at public gatherings, hosting a neighborhood activity, etc.), but otherwise the two are coexistent and support each other.

Loosely	Tightly
Integrated - - - - - - - - - Integrated	
Symbolic	Controlling
Presence	Presence

More of the CCDO networks of organizations are tightly integrated for two reasons.

1. Dispensational theology drives some to see good works and social change as the medium for evangelism. In these contexts it is desirable for the church to retain a controlling interest in the program formation and practices of the CCDO.

2. Most of them grew out of a single congregation's desire to make a lasting impact in their parish community. The members have and hold the vision for change in the community. The CCDO is their vehicle to cause desired changes. They are reticent to diversify their board control.

Reformed Christians embrace a worldview in which all social systems and structures are subject to the reign of God. Reformed Christians commit to the transformation of the full range of social structures. They love to see Christians work at social justice at all levels. They do not insist on church control of community programs, but they encourage church member infiltration and they look for their redemptive impact in all community organizations.

Reformed Christians do not embrace a theology of good works only for evangelism purposes; they stress the importance of bringing the message of salvation along with deeds that bring God's grace to needy people. Changed hearts are as important to them as changed structures. They recognize that long-term, caring relationships between Christians and unchurched people are at the heart of effective evangelism. Often they are also at the heart of helping people make sustainable behavioral changes. Programs for social change bring opportunity for these relationships, so they like to see the church involved in these types of programs. Reformed Christians can probably be comfortable anywhere on this spectrum but will tend to be toward the center.

Three primary reasons explain why churches do not run community development programs:

- Church/state separation laws would be compromised.

- Funding sources from business, foundation, and government sources would be less accessible due to perceived values compromises.

- Many churches do not have the necessary organizational flexibility and responsiveness to run CCDOs range of programs.

Christian Community Development CRWRC Style

CRWRC finds that most Christian community developers once assumed they had something to give away to poor people (knowledge, education, skills, goods, or services). They learned, however, to avoid this approach. Rather than assume poor people need external resources for change, they now assume poor people have all that they need to help themselves. The inter-

ventionist helps people attain their dreams or discover their own solutions to problems they choose to work on. CRWRC believes community development work has little to do with adding relief and services to a community. Instead, this work unwraps the covers that hide or bind people from using their own skills, energies, and resources in solving problems and attaining dreams.

Development implies capacity. People have the capacity to reach their desired state. Development builds up what is latent in the community.

Development focuses on goals and the future.

Development empowers people to do what they can and want to do.

Development is a process (not a program) that continues once it is understood and practiced. It becomes a way of life in the community.

Development is growth, improvement, or maturity as perceived by the end-users.

Development is relationships among people in a community who want the same future.

Development is helping people become stakeholders in their communities.

Community development can begin only when the people of the community convene to discuss what they want to be different. This, more than anything else, is the piece that is missing in most North American community development efforts.

While community development rarely begins without an interventionist beginning the work in a community, the interventionist can rarely be the visible change agent in the community. The most successful interventionists begin by supporting and partnering with a resident change agent from within the community.

What Do CCDO Programs Look Like?

No two CCDO programs are identical. Each one's journey began differently. Most CCDOs have a mix of the following program components:

- Spiritual Formation (through mentors, small groups, Bible studies, prayer, worship)
- Direct Service:

  Food distribution

  Clothing distribution

  Transportation

- Health Services (especially that focus on children, pregnant women, and elderly people)
- Youth Programs (especially childcare and alternatives to gangs)
- Empowerment Groups (AA, Single Parent Support, Next Step)
- Income Generation:

  Employment training and preparation

  Job referral and placement

  Microenterprise

  New business starts

  Attracting new business to the area

  Bringing basic service institutions to the area (banks, grocery stores, etc.)

- Education:

  Literacy and libraries

  School support programs (especially tutoring programs)

  Computer training

Preschools and alternative schools

Adult education

- Legal Services
- Housing:

  Transitional housing

  Housing repair

  New housing development

  Attracting homeowners (from diverse economic levels)

  Affordable rental units

  Landlord-tenant mediation

  Seniors housing

- Social Justice Activities:

  Racial reconciliation (events and programs)

  Representation of residents on public boards

  Residency requirements for public servants

  Voter registration

- Social Action:

  Community organization to fight violence and drug use

  Crime-prevention activities

All of these programs tend to be undergirded by an intake system designed to help people articulate their dreams for the future, diagnose barriers, and plan incremental steps to sustainable changes. Individual or group mentoring usually strengthens a person's resolve to make sustainable planned change.

To look at this another way, think of widening spheres of community development:

1. At the heart of community development lies an intake process in which individuals and families express their immediate needs and are brought through a diagnostic process that helps them identify some long-term goals and dreams.

2. The second sphere is direct service, in which individuals/families are directed to resources available to them in health care, food supplements, rent assistance, appliance repair or distribution, transportation, and clothing distribution. The community development organization may run many of these services itself and even use them as training and employment opportunities for local residents.

3. The third sphere of service is personal empowerment, in which individuals and families are directed to resources available to them for personal and group support (single-parent support groups, AA and twelve-step groups, and spiritual nurture groups). Again the community development organization may provide Christian groups for these purposes. It may also work with local congregations that provide these as side-door ministries of the church.

4. The fourth sphere of service is community empowerment, in which individuals/families participate in income generation and employment activities, education opportunities, youth activities, legal services, and home ownership in the community. This sphere also harnesses economic institutions (banks, grocery stores, service organizations, etc.) to reinvest in the community.

All these services should be present and should result in a stable community. The impact of these services should result in the individual and family becoming stakeholders in their community, keeping every possible dollar changing hands in the community. Many resources for these services will be brokered directly by the community development organization. Some will be offered by the CCDO through joint venture type agreements with other institutions.

5. The fifth sphere of service is creating community identity. People today do not interact with, or even know, their neighbors; life goes on behind closed doors. Community identity requires spending time with neighbors. In this sphere the community development organization invites residents to

- participate in community celebration activities and events (groundbreaking on a new house in the neighborhood, dedication ceremonies, three-on-three basketball tournaments).

- celebrate community holidays together.

- participate in racial reconciliation events.

- participate in activities that create community pride (recognition events for a community resident who accomplishes a milestone), or a day to clean up the park, or a community call to stand vigil to eradicate a crack house in the community.

- participate in providing community services ("barn-raising" activities for the community).

6. The final sphere of service is organizing the community to influence and even take control of the institutions that control the community:

- Work with police to make the community a safe place to live.

- Articulate community values and express them at city council meetings.

- Elect local residents to the boards of public institutions that impact the community.

- Pass residency requirements for the community's service providers (police, ambulance, firefighters, health workers, teachers).

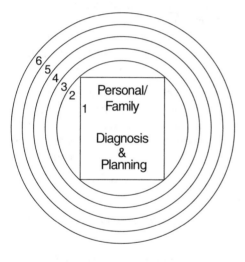

This diagram represents the spheres of community development. Operating in as many of these spheres as possible is important, even if the scope of services in each sphere is somewhat limited at first. The best CCDOs network well with the established organizations providing these services. They also ensure that these services are recognized and accessible in their community under their own name.

Successful community organizing must raise local residents to be the leaders in all these spheres of activity; therefore, leadership development must be a key function of the organization from the beginning.

How much of this work can a church do? Few Christian Reformed churches have accomplished significant results in the fourth, fifth, or sixth spheres without working with or through a Christian Community Development Organization. Few conversions have stemmed from CCDOs that are not closely linked with an anchor church. Spiritual formation grows with the involvement of church members in CCDOs. Churches grow through their involvement with CCDOs.

Can you picture a vibrant, healthy community in which people help one another flourish? Can you envision a vibrant, adaptive church at the heart of this change, supporting and partnering with the CCDO to create the vision of Christian community? Churches that want to bring sustainable changes to their communities will create new CCDOs or partner with existing ones.

The kingdom of God is here now. Christians have been fully vested and fully empowered to make this world more like heaven to poor and needy people. We lack nothing now that we will have in heaven. Our lack of faith, our lack of creativity, and our lack of commitment are what hold us back.

The time has come to pray, be creative, and let the mission shape the church's organizational life as it responds to God's call to be merciful and to usher in the fullness of his kingdom.

Appendix A

Scripture Passages For Deacons

These are some selected texts that relate to God's heart and mandate for ministries of mercy.

This list is not exhaustive. The passages are not listed in any order or priority. For deacons who are searching, the list may be a good place to start.

Exodus 22:21-22

Leviticus 19:9-10

Deuteronomy 16:9-12; 24:17-22

Psalm 41:1; 112:4, 5, 9; 146:7-9

Proverbs 14:20-21; 28:27

Isaiah 3:13-15; 58:5-7

Jeremiah 7:5-6

Ezekiel 22:7, 29

Amos 2:6, 7; 8:4-7

Micah 2:2

Zechariah 7:9, 10

Matthew 10:34-42; 18:32-34; 19:16-30; 25:31-46

Luke 1:51-53; 3:8-14; 4:18; 6:32-36; 12:30-34; 18:22-30

John 14:12-14

Acts 4:32-34

Romans 15:26-28

2 Corinthians 5:18-20; 8, 9

Galatians 2:10

Philippians 2:1-13

Colossians 3: 12-17

1 Timothy 3:8-13; 6:17-19

Hebrews 13:2, 13-16

James 1:27; 2:14-17, 22-27; 4:17; 5:11

1 John 3:16-18

Appendix B

Various Articles from the 1995 Church Order

Article 25b

The elders, with the minister(s), shall oversee the doctrine and life of the members of the congregation and fellow officebearers, shall exercise admonition and discipline along with pastoral care of the congregation, shall participate in and promote evangelism, and shall defend the faith.

Article 25c

The deacons shall represent and administer the mercy of Christ to all people, especially to those who belong to the community of believers, and shall stimulate the members of Christ's church to faithful, obedient stewardship of their resources on behalf of the needy—all with words of biblical encouragement and testimony which assure the unity of word and deed.

Article 74

a. Each church shall bring the gospel to unbelievers in its own community. This task shall be sponsored and governed by the council. This task may be executed, when conditions warrant, in cooperation with one or more neighboring churches.

b. Each church shall carry on a ministry of mercy. The deacons shall enable the needy under their care to make use of Christian institutions of mercy. They shall confer and cooperate with diaconates of neighboring churches when this is de-

sirable for the proper performance of their task. They may also seek mutual understandings with agencies in their community which are caring for the needy, so that the gifts may be distributed properly.

Article 75

a. The classes shall, whenever necessary, assist the churches in their local evangelistic programs. The classes themselves may perform this work of evangelism when it is beyond the scope and resources of the local churches. To administer these tasks each classis shall have a classical home missions committee.

b. The classes shall, whenever necessary, assist the churches in their ministry of mercy. The classes themselves may perform this ministry when it is beyond the scope and resources of the local churches. To administer this task each classis shall have a classical diaconal committee.

Article 76

a. Synod shall encourage and assist congregations and classes in their work of evangelism, and shall also carry on such home missions activities as are beyond their scope and resources. To administer these activities synod shall appoint a denominational home missions committee, whose work shall be controlled by synodical regulations.

b. Synod shall encourage and assist congregations and classes in their ministry of mercy, and shall carry on such work as is beyond their scope and resources. Synod shall appoint a diaconal committee to administer the denominational ministry of mercy. The work of this committee shall be governed by synodical regulations.

Article 77

a. Synod shall determine the field in which the joint world mission work of the churches is to be carried on, regulate the manner in which this task is to be performed, provide for its cooperative support, and encourage the congregations to call and support missionaries. To administer these activities synod shall appoint a denominational world missions committee, whose work shall be controlled by synodical regulations.

b. The denominational diaconal committee shall extend the ministry of mercy of the congregations and classes worldwide.

Appendix C

**Form for the
Ordination of Elders and Deacons**

(The Deacons Portion)

(Approved by Christian Reformed
Church Synod 1982)

In the officebearers of the church we see the love of Christ for his people. As the Lord of the church he appoints leaders and by his Spirit equips them so that believers may grow in faith, develop disciplined Christian living, serve others in selfless love, and share with all the good news of salvation. He taught us the spirit of true leadership when he said, "Whoever would be great among you must be your servant, and whoever would be first among you must be your slave; even as the Son of Man came not to be served but to serve, and to give his life as a ransom for many" (Matt. 20:26-28).

Deacons serve by showing mercy to the church and to all people. They received this task in the early church when the apostles designated special persons for the work of mercy (Acts 6:1-6; 2 Cor. 8-9). The deacons stimulate relief in Christ's name for the poor, the distressed, and the victims of injustice. Thereby they show that Christians live by the Spirit of the kingdom, fervently desiring to give life the shape of things to come. Deacons are therefore called to assess needs, promote stewardship and hospitality, collect and disburse resources for benevolence, and develop programs of assistance. They are also called to speak words of Christian encouragement. Thus, in word as well as in deed they demonstrate the care of the Lord himself.

Charge to the Deacons

I charge you, deacons, to inspire faithful stewardship in this congregation. Remind us that "everyone to whom much is given, of him will much be required" (Luke 12:48b). Teach us to be merciful. Prompt us to seize new opportunities to worship God with offerings of wealth, time, and ability. Realize that benevolence is a quality of our life in Christ, and not merely a matter of financial assistance. Therefore, minister to rich and poor alike, both within and outside the church. Weigh the needs of causes, and use this church's resources discerningly. Be compassionate to the needy. Encourage them with words that create hope in their hearts and with deeds that bring joy into their lives. Be prophetic critics of the waste, injustice, and selfishness in society, and be sensitive counselors to the victims of such evils. Let your lives be above reproach; live as examples of Christ Jesus; look to the interests of others.

Appendix D

Synodical Reports for Study

1. Synodical Report 1973, Report 44 on Office and Ordination

This report examines why the church needs offices, how they relate to the office of believer, and how the offices relate to each other. The final summary states that offices are gifts of God to his church. Each office exists to equip the saints for their service. Offices stand side by side according to function and none is more important to the church than another.

2. Synodical Report 1981, Report 32 on Studies on Women in Office

Part III: The Office of Deacon pp. 495-512

Included in this report on women in office is a very brief but helpful overview of the history of the office of deacon in the Reformed tradition. In conclusion, it suggests that while there have been different accents or nuances of function over the years in the office of deacon, the lasting legacy of deacons in the Reformed tradition is ministries of mercy.

Appendix E

Types of Diaconal Ministry

1. **Target ministries** (paper-products ministry, refugee ministry, abuse ministry, homeless ministry, employment ministry, budgeting ministry, transportation ministry).

2. **Recovery ministries** (divorce recovery groups and twelve-step recovery groups—AA, NA, Overeaters, Overspenders).

3. **One-to-one ministry linkages** in which church members are paired with needy families for support and assistance in following mutually arranged plans to accomplish their dreams.

4. **Next-step groups** to bring together needy individuals and families who share a desire to help one another accomplish their dreams. These groups provide support, self-help networking, accountability, and Bible study. On occasion they also engage in cooperative income-generating and cost-saving activities and pooled income ventures. Associations of these small groups can even develop political power to garner needed services.

5. **Cooperative projects** with other diaconates/churches to meet needs that are too big for one single church to handle. (This is a key component of diaconal conferences, which work with churches in close geographic proximity.)

6. **Emergency relief** (benevolence) to families in crisis.

7. **Referral and advocacy services** to garner support from external sources to help people find solutions to their problems and resources for their dreams.

Appendix F

Concentric Circles of Service

December 12, 1991

Deacons have a wide arena of responsibility—helping their church members bring Christ's mercy to this broken world.

The following are the arenas of responsibility, adapted from *The Deacons Handbook* by Berghoef and De Koster, Christian's Library Press, Grand Rapids, MI; ISBN 0-934874-01-8.

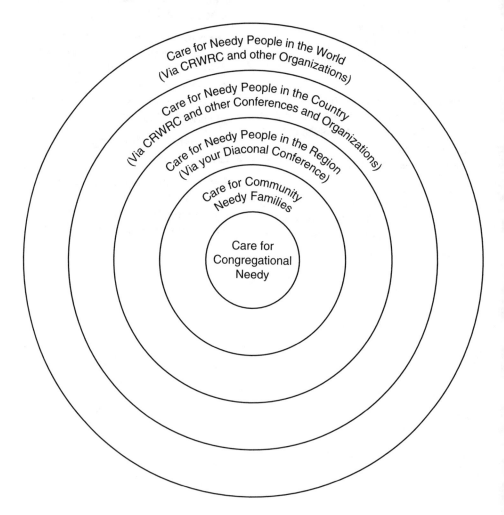

Care for Needy People in the World
(Via CRWRC and other Organizations)

Care for Needy People in the Country
(Via CRWRC and other Conferences and Organizations)

Care for Needy People in the Region
(Via your Diaconal Conference)

Care for Community
Needy Families

Care for
Congregational
Needy

Appendix G

A Community Needs Assessment

A preliminary needs assessment includes the following questions for church leaders and community organizations:

1. Whom do you serve? Describe your target population.

2. What additional human needs do they have that you do not meet? Do certain needs arise repeatedly among those you serve?

3. Do you know of any major changes coming in the service delivery system to your target population?

4. What can ordinary church volunteers or a faith community do that would meet strategic needs in your target population's lives?

Educational institutions, medical/health organizations, mental health organizations, geriatric organizations, social service organizations, police, and courts are great places to begin with these questions.

Appendix H

Criteria for a Vision Statement

Characteristics of Vision:

- Specific
- Detailed
- Narrows the focus
- Actionable
- Practical
- Strategic
- Change-oriented
- Empowering for service
- Makes you unique
- Articulated by the leader
- Emphasis on people
- Inspiring

Keys to an Effective Vision Statement:

- Twenty-five words or less
- Nonpreachy and nontechnical language
- Concise concept
- Precise wording
- Memorable but not trite
- Intimately tied to teaching, programs, and leadership efforts
- Inspires excitement and commitment
- Clarifies direction
- Reflects ambition

A Vision Checklist:

- Focused on the future
- Clear and easily understandable
- Brief
- A reflection of what God wants
- Identifies your distinctive mission
- Inspires your staff and constituents
- Realistic and challenging
- Fully owned by the leader
- Action oriented
- Provides a specific direction
- Reduces the ministry opportunities you accept
- Consistent with your mission
- Consistent with your past
- Strategic
- Make change more palatable

Examples of Diaconal Vision Statements:

1. To help poor and needy people in Georgetown through one-to-one ministries, small group ministries, and church-based community projects.

2. To respond to Madison community's pain, poverty, and system injustices so that poor and needy people are reconciled to God, each other, and themselves.

3. To deploy and support members in ministries of mercy by

- creating a flow of screened poor and needy people.

- increasing church-based target and side-door ministries.

- linking members with denominational agencies for regional, national and international ministry opportunities.

4. To serve the Vietnamese refugee community in Holland and the seniors in the church so that they make appropriate transitions in their lives.

Examples of Church Vision Statements:

1. To equip professionals in New York City to impact their web of relationships by reaching nonbelievers through cell groups and marketplace ministries that address urban needs.

2. To build a network of neighborhood churches within the metroplex, working in cooperation with other ministries to restore ethnic unity and family strength.

3. To penetrate Central America with the gospel by using our resources to develop homegrown missionaries who partner with indigenous believers.

4. To offer physical care, personal attention, and practical teaching that satisfies the needs of senior citizens in our town.

5. To develop Christian self-help groups so that everyone in Cascade Township has access to support in taking next steps in their lives.

General Comments About Vision:

1. Consensus results from vision among the church's leaders, not vice versa. Vision does not come from consensus.

2. Real leaders are visionaries—leadership does not occur without vision.

3. Vision creates the future (doesn't set boundaries).

4. Vision puts the church at risk because it is about change.

5. The goal of vision is faithfulness to God's preferred future.

6. Vision motivates a church to move; it does not force change.

7. Vision is unique, like a fingerprint.

8. Capturing God's vision can take months of input, study, and reflection.

9. Vision is not a temporary change. It is a directional change (shouldn't change every two or three years.)

Adapted from *Understanding Ministry in a Changing Culture,* a workshop by George Barna. © 1994 by the Barna Research Group Ltd., Glendale, California.

Appendix I

Monthly Deacons Report

Deacon's Name_____

Month _____

1. List the names of any church members who helped you in your diaconal work this month.

2. List all of the households you helped (or had someone help) this month. Briefly describe how they were helped.

3. Please place an asterisk (*) beside the names of all nonmember households.

4. Place an X besides the names of all households who reached stage three or beyond this month. See stages in next column. These households are being helped to *solve* their disabling problems.

5. What frustrations, barriers, or problems did you face this month as deacon?

6. What recommendations would you like to bring to the diaconate? Please include your reasons and list some positive and negative consequences your recommendation might have if implemented.

7. What training or education do you or church members need to become more effective in your ministries of mercy?

8. Please circle your morale as a deacon for this month: low good high

Stages Towards Self-Sufficiency

Stage 1. A deacon or volunteer agrees to help the household.

Stage 2. Immediate aid is given to get the household beyond crisis.

Stage 3. The household defines problems and sets goals that reflect its hopes and dreams.

Stage 4. The household is able to identify tasks and opportunities that will get it beyond its current problems and accomplish its goals.

Stage 5. Agreements are reached about what the household will do to achieve its goals and what the church will do to help the household achieve these goals.

Stage 6. Regular meeting times are set to build friendship and monitor goal attainment (daily, weekly, monthly).

Stage 7. The household helps someone else under the supervision of the deacons.

Appendix J

Target and Side-Door Ministries

AA, NA, Al-Anon. (Churches rent space to these national programs.)

Abuse Survivors Support Group

Aerobics. (Aerobics class with licensed instructor held in church building.)

Adult Reading Program Improvement

After-School Youth Club

AIDS Support Group

Baby Crib Ministry. (Crib with bedding and layette delivered and set up in homes.)

Blood Pressure Screening and Blood Drives

Big Brother/Sister Program. (Mentoring program for youth.)

Cancer Support Group

Child Safety Kits. (Assembled by church and distributed via the Health Department.)

Christian Home for Pregnant Single Women

Christian Singles Support Group

Clothing Redistribution

Couples With Kids. (Parenting support group.)

Daycare Ministry

Dresser Ministry. (Dresser filled with baby items given to low-income moms.)

Financial Counseling

Food Pantry

Friendship Ministry. (Social/spiritual program for persons with disabilities.)

Furniture Ministry

Head Start Child Care

Latch-Key Program

Manage Your Money Seminars

Marriage Enrichment Series

Moms Night Out. (Special night out featuring devotions and craft targeting community women.)

Paper Product Ministry. (Supplemental aid to low-income families.)

Preschool Program

Rainbows for All God's Children. (Support group for children who have suffered loss of parent through divorce or death.)

Respite Program. (Volunteers care for persons with special needs, providing a needed break for careproviders.)

Restore. (Partnering as friends with ex-prisoners.)

Shelter for Abused Women and Children

Single Parent Counseling

Single Parent Support group

Support Group for Dysfunctional Families

Support Group for Parents of Special Needs Children

Tel-A-Care. (Daily calling ministry to check on seniors who live alone.)

Transitional Housing

Transportation Ministry. (Auto repairs, car purchase program for low-income families.)

Tutoring

Widow/Widower Support Group

Women to Women. (Six-week series of events for growth/nurture.)

Women Ministry Support Group

Youth Hockey. (Recreational program for church and community youth.)

Appendix K

Resources for Teaching Biblical Financial Living

Each of the organizations listed below offer excellent books, videos, and study materials to help people discover contentment through biblically faithful financial living.

1. FirstFruits
   The Barnabas Foundation
   15127 S. 73rd St., Suite G
   Orland Park, IL 60462
   (708) 532-3444

2. Crown Ministries, Inc.
   530 Crown Oak Centre Dr.
   Longwood, FL 32750
   (407) 331-6000

3. Larry Burkett
   Christian Financial Concepts
   P.O. Box 2377
   Gainesville, GA 30503-2377
   (404) 534-1000

4. Ron Blue
   Walk Through the Bible Ministries
   61 Perimeter Park NE
   P.O. Box 80587
   Atlanta, GA 30366
   (414) 458-9300

Appendix L

Ministry Plan

Church Deacon: _____

_____

Address: _____

_____

_____

_____

Phone: _____

_____

_____

Family Served: _____

_____

Address: _____

_____

_____

_____

Phone: _____

_____

_____

Part One: Mentor

Most people cannot make major changes in their lives without active support from a friend or accountability partner. We call this person a *mentor.* This part of the plan simply lists the name of the person who has been selected on the basis of his/her desire to be a mentor to someone who wants help. He/she has promised to:

- Pray daily for you.

- Meet with you face-to-face on a weekly basis for not less than one hour for support, friendship, and guidance.

- Handle any information you share with great care to keep your name and reputation strong.

Name of Mentor: _____

Address: _____

_____

_____

_____

Phone: _____

_____

Part Two: Immediate Aid Agreed To and Given

Many people want the church or an organization to make their problems disappear. We do not believe that this will help you in the long run. Your choices and actions were part of what got you to this point of need. You must be responsible to solve past problems and create your new future. The use of immediate aid is to help you move just far enough from crisis that you can take the opportunity to plan and dream about your future and what you want to accomplish in it. Our aid will not solve all of your problems. The best we can do is take the hurtful edge off your current problems and partner with you to find creative ways to manage your future.

Date: Describe Aid Given:

_____   _____

_____   _____

_____   _____

_____   _____

_____   _____

Part Three: Goals

Lasting help for most people comes in the form of a partnership. The first piece of the partnership is deciding what the goal or end result of the partnership will be. It must be your realistic dream for your preferred future—your goals for yourself. What would you like to have accomplished three months, six months, twelve months, or five years from now? Think in terms of housing, work, education, home life, security, children, spiritual life, friends, income range, skills, and resources.

Write down goals that reflect your hopes and dreams for your future, with time lines for goal attainment.

1.

2.

3.

4.

5.

Part Four: Problems

You have not been able to achieve these goals so far in your life. What are some of the problems that might prevent you from achieving your goals in the future? It might be helpful to list them under the categories below. Try to list very specifically the root problems that will likely make it difficult for you to attain the goals you wrote above.

Lack of Encouragement or Support:

Lack of Information:

Lack of Skills:

Lack of Resources:

Other:

Part Five: Financial Information

Fill out the following financial information form, using documentation whenever possible.

MONTHLY INCOME:

Sources: Amounts:

Employer(s)   _____
Child Support   _____
Alimony   _____
General Assistance   _____
Government Assistance   _____
Social Security/Insurance   _____
Pension   _____
Disability Insurance   _____
Other   _____
                                  _____
                                  _____

TOTAL INCOME   _____

MONTHLY INCOME   _____
FIXED EXPENSES/MO.   _____
VARIABLE EXP/MO.   _____
TOTAL SAVINGS   _____

LIST ALL OUTSTANDING DEBTS

         Vendor   Amount

1.

2.

3.

4.

5.

Maintain one account for fixed expenses and a separate account for variable expenses.

FIXED EXPENSES:

Monthly Church Budget   _____

Housing
a. Rent
b. Mortgage   _____
c. Taxes/assess   _____
d. Insurance   _____

Utilities
a. Electric
b. Gas or Oil   _____
c. Water   _____
d. Sewer   _____
e. Garbage   _____

Transportation
a. Car Payments
b. Licenses   _____
c. Car Insurance   _____
d. Gas   _____
e. Repairs   _____
f. Bus Fares   _____

Medical Care
a. Doctor Fees
b. Dental & Ortho   _____
c. Medications   _____
d. Counseling   _____
e. Insurance   _____

Life Insurance   _____

Childcare   _____

TOTAL MONTHLY   _____

FIXED EXPENSES   _____

VARIABLE EXPENSES:

Monthly Food

a. Groceries _____

b. Restaurants _____

c. Tobacco _____

Telephone _____

Personal Care

a. Barber/Parlor _____

b. Toiletries _____

c. Cosmetics _____

Recreation _____

a. Movies _____

b. Hobbies _____

c. Vacations _____

d. Cable TV _____

e. Newspapers _____

f. Magazines _____

g. Gifts _____

h. Other _____

_____

Education

a. Tuition/Fees _____

b. Books/Supplies _____

Furnishings

a. Appliances _____

b. Furniture _____

c. Other _____

_____

_____

Clothing _____

Shoes _____

Laundry _____

TOTAL MONTHLY _____

VARIABLE EXPENSES _____

Part Six: Skills

Many people who need help are also willing to help others out of the thankfulness for the help they received. List hobbies, talents, and skills you could use to serve others when that time comes for you.

_____

_____

_____

_____

_____

_____

_____

_____

_____

_____

_____

_____

_____

Part Seven: Commitment

Our partnership with you is to help you meet your goals listed above. The next step is to decide some steps you can take to move towards attaining those goals. Because we want to help you attain those goals, we will write down what you can count on from us to help you achieve them. Most of our help will be nonfinancial. It will help you access information you need and services that are available to you to help you meet your goals. Any financial assistance will be directed at helping you create **new opportunities** for yourself. They will not be directed at problems.

Remember you can count on your mentor to pray for you daily and to meet with you regularly to support you. On a separate sheet of paper write down (together) all the sequential steps it will take to meet each goal. Tell us what you can do for each step and we will decide what we can do to help:

What will you do to attain your goals?

1.

2.

3.

4.

5.

6.

7.

8.

9.

10.

What will the mentor and church community do to help?

1.

2.

3.

4.

5.

6.

7.

8.

9.

10.

Note: If you do not fulfill your end of this agreement, we cannot fulfill our end of it. If you have good reasons for not following through on the plan, we can always renegotiate this plan around different goals or steps. Our help depends on your taking action for your future.

Part Eight: Evaluation

We want to be fair to you and provide all the encouragement, help, and support you need to attain your goals. We need, therefore, to evaluate regularly whether this is the right plan for you and whether we are on track with it. Most people find that it needs to be amended or "tweaked" at various times. It is usually helpful to monitor it frequently at first and then less frequently when all is going well according to plan.

Progress in Goal / Dream Attainment will be reviewed:

____ Daily   ____ Weekly   ____ Monthly

Other Conditions of Agreement:

Signed _____
Date _____

Signed _____
Date _____

Appendix M

Christian Community Development Association

What Is It?

The Christian Community Development Association of Christian Community Development Organizations was started by Dr. John Perkins. He, along with Mary Nelson (Bethel New Life), Wayne Gordon (Lawndale Christian Community), Bob Lupton (FCS Urban Ministries), Glenn Kehrein (Circle Urban Ministries), and over one hundred and fifty other ministries have formed the Christian Community Development Association. The CCDA is based on three core biblical bases for community development:

1. Reconciliation

Reconciliation with God—finding new life with God, living his way.

Racial reconciliation—renewing the fabric of community so that all people can live harmoniously drawing on the strengths of each person and culture.

2. Redistribution

Rebuilding the community economic infrastructure so that once again residents' dollars circulate in their community repeatedly.

Harnessing market forces so that opportunity for economic prosperity comes to urban communities.

Sharing the wealth of the rich with the poor and the strengths of the poor with the rich.

Sharing leadership by developing local residents to be the leaders in their communities.

3. Relocation

Change in urban communities has to begin from within them. Residents of urban communities have gifts, energies, and passion to change their own communities. Community development builds on their vision and initiatives.

Isolation of poor from middle- and upper-income families leads to widening the gap between rich and poor. Healthy urban neighborhoods reweave the fabric of community around a diversity of people from all income levels.

Change agents can rarely be effective in communities where they do not live. A Christian Community Developer must earn his neighbors' respect through his presence, modeling, and message of change.